Stealing First

Stealing First
The Teddy Kremer Story

Teddy Kremer

with Diane Lang & Michael Buchanan

Deeds Publishing | Atlanta

Published by Deeds Publishing in Athens, GA
www.deedspublishing.com

Printed in The United States of America

Cover artwork and text layout by Mark Babcock

Library of Congress Cataloging-in-Publications data is available upon request.

ISBN 978-1-944193-06-5

Books are available in quantity for promotional or premium use. For information, email info@deedspublishing.com.

First Edition, 2016

10 9 8 7 6 5 4 3 2 1

*To all people with disabilities and special needs around the world,
we thank you for being a beautiful part of our lives.*

Acknowledgements

THIS BOOK'S JOURNEY INVOLVES MANY PEOPLE TO WHOM WE OWE much gratitude. First and foremost is Teddy Kremer, the good luck charm for the Cincinnati Reds. We thank him for the joy, enthusiasm and whole-hearted support he brought to this project. To some people, he has accomplished the impossible. But once you know Teddy, you realize he is only being Teddy, a person who defies limitations.

Teddy's parents, Cheryl and Dave Kremer, and his brother, David, have been exceptional in sharing with us their "Teddy stories." When we needed to clarify events in Teddy's life, they willingly gave up endless hours to help us with Teddy's story. Other relatives and his multitude of friends, especially the Roedersheimer family, shared insights into Teddy's life and personality. His teachers, coaches and classmates at Mercy Montessori and Colerain High School added flavor, humor and drama to Teddy's days in school. Others who contributed to our understanding of Teddy, include his co-workers at 5th 3rd Bank and Hillcrest; his mentors at Project Search; and his softball, swimming and dancing coaches.

We are especially thankful to John Erardi, the *Cincinnati Enquirer* sportswriter whose story about Teddy's batboy experience ran on the front page of the paper in September of 2012. Because of John's story and Jeff Swinger's remarkable photos, Teddy and others with Down syndrome now have a voice. We are especially thankful to John Erardi for writing the foreword to this book.

And, we would be remiss without thanking Teddy's friend and favorite ballplayer Todd Frazier for befriending Teddy and welcoming him with outstretched arms. Literally! We also thank Manager Dusty Baker and fan Bill Hemmer of FOX News for their eagerness to endorse *Stealing First.*

We also give thanks to movie director Jason Winn, who told us to "go watch a story on ABC News about a batboy," and Craig Lindvahl, the filmmaker who first connected us with the Kremers.

As with all of our creative endeavors, the support of our families is important beyond measure. We thank them for their unyielding support for and belief in our work.

Finally, we would like to acknowledge Phil and Bob Castellini of the Cincinnati Reds for taking a leap of faith and giving Teddy the chance of a lifetime. That simple act of kindness will resonate for a long time with those who have been told that some things are impossible. Who ever thought that a batboy could mean so much to a city, a team and its fans? Thanks again, Teddy, for enhancing our lives with your gift of joy.

Foreword

WHEN I FIRST SAW JEFF SWINGER'S COOL PHOTO OF REDS SECOND baseman Brandon Phillips looking backward with a huge smile toward the batboy, it made me smile, too.

Just as it no doubt made thousands of other readers of the *Cincinnati Enquirer* smile that morning.

I don't recall thinking, *I wonder if there's a story here.*

For me, it was just another great Jeff Swinger photo.

But when Jeff came to me a few days later and said, "Something was happening in there," I knew he meant the clubhouse and dugout, the inner sanctum, the team psyche and soul.

"Got them down to the very marrow," to paraphrase the blue-eyed Irish soul singer Van Morrison.

I set forth to try to re-create what Jeff had witnessed; I hadn't been there that night. I trusted Jeff's sixth sense. Having worked with him on several in-depth pieces, I knew that he had a good eye not only for what he was shooting, but for the story itself.

I'd been writing human interest stories for almost four decades at the *Enquirer*, some in Metro and the Features sections, most in Sports. The only thing they had in common was a glimpse into the ways people affect other people, that is, in how we all relate.

In particular, I knew the effect that the Ted Kremers of the world have; my wife, Barb, is a special education teacher, and she played a critical role in my understanding of Down syndrome. I was constantly bouncing things off her as I was working on the story.

Several of the young people I've profiled in-depth over the years, young people making their way in the world—St. Bernard basketball player Nick Mosley, Hillsboro wrestler Dustin Carter,

St. Rita's/Winton Woods/Ohio State golfer Kevin Hall, DePaul Cristo Rey basketball player Darrion Arnold, among them—have rubbed off on me in a good way; inspired me, in other words.

Ted had this same effect. Normally I'm reserved, not one to easily let my guard down around strangers. But around Ted, there *are* no strangers. I could be myself almost instantaneously, no self-consciousness, no worries. Just like around family and friends.

You're in Ted's world now, dude; no boundaries, be yourself, let 'er rip.

I saw the same thing in so many of the Reds players. Some of them wary, even standoffish with people they didn't know, but they were drawn magically into Ted's world. Soon, everybody was laughing. I interviewed them weeks after these dugout and clubhouse encounters, and their faces lit up.

The "Teddy Effect" is what Swinger and I called it; fellow former *Enquirer* colleague Glenn Hartong produced another of his terrific videos on it, titling it one and the same.

As I attempted to re-create Ted's first night in the Reds dugout, I wrestled with the best way to tell the story. I settled on what should have seemed obvious, but at the time wasn't at all: Ted's effect on the players. Former Reds pitcher Bronson Arroyo later told me that of all the major league clubhouse he'd been in—and there are many—"The most difficult thing I've seen is for an outsider to be comfortable."

"Ted was that from the moment he walked in. He wanted you to know that he knew you, who you were and what you'd done.

"'Hey, Bronson Arroyo, you've'—throw in any stat; Ted knows 'em all—'done such-and-so, I'm going to be watching you tonight. I'm behind you man!' And he did that with everybody. He'd bring the Latinos into it, too. Ted'd go back-and-forth with (Johnny) Cueto. Ted knew his stats, too. He knew everybody on the team and in the organization.

"And if you were 'down' (emotionally, in the dugout, after not having come through in some situation), he'd buck you up. 'I got your back, man. You can do this; you'll get 'em next time; don't let it get you down.'

"That's the kind of unconditional support a good manager and pitching coach gives. The reason Ted fits in so well is that he's so comfortable in his own skin. He has no agenda, and people can see that right away; they don't wonder, *What's this guy's agenda; what's he after?*"

Arroyo, it could be said, was channeling Ted before he ever knew him. In my 30 years of covering the Reds, Arroyo is the most honest, forthright, transparent player I've ever met. He didn't articulate to me why he went to the trouble of calling me for this foreword when I had reached out to him, but clearly, that was it: Teddy Ballgame is a clubhouse paragon, the virtual "good teammate." He fits in.

Another former Red, Chris Heisey, had said as much when I began work on the Ted story, "He's always smiling, always joking, always having fun. Everybody likes being around somebody like that. He's cool. I wish he'd come back more."

I've compared Ted to the most genuine of politicians in the way he works a room, totally natural. I've said—and meant—that Ted could be elected mayor of Cincinnati (or, at least, Todd Frazier's secretary of goodwill and camaraderie).

There isn't an organization, business or team in the world that wouldn't be better with Ted in it. He's as recognizable around town as any Red or Bengal, and I've seen people notice him who I wouldn't think would notice anybody, and watched them ask Ted to pose for a photo with them or ask for his autograph. And Ted is always happy to oblige. He relishes his celebrity, unlike many athletes I've met who are uncomfortable in that light. (That's OK, fellas; just emulate Ted.)

I've heard stories about restaurateurs who don't take reservations take them when they hear third-hand that Ted is in the party. When his family went to pick up the cake for his surprise 30th birthday party, and the clerk saw the name "Ted" scripted into the icing, she asked, "Is this *the* Ted?" I've heard Mr. Castellini himself, the Reds owner, call for a "Ted infusion" in the dugout.

I didn't think there was anything extraordinary about the story when I submitted it. It was one of the easiest stories I've ever written, just a matter of finding the right transitions and dropping in the Ted pearls.

Greg Noble, the best sports editor I ever had, gave me the best advice I had ever received and I always followed it to a T: "Stories are like fastballs. There's always another one coming. Take your swing and get ready for the next one."

But a funny thing happened as I was getting ready for the next one.

By the time I checked my computer the day the story ran, the emails, texts and posts were piling up. The outpouring for Ted's story was overwhelming; I'd received over 150 personal contacts.

I'd been tipped off the story would be running on Page One on that Sunday in the *Enquirer*—Sept. 17, 2012—but I didn't tell the Kremers; I just generally let them know it was coming. The main reason I didn't specify the date is because too often I've seen feature stories get bumped for lack of space or breaking news. For the same reason, I didn't mention Page One to them.

Besides, I like surprises (on *other* people, that is).

That morning, Ted's father, Dave, received a phone call from his sister, Sue: "Have you seen the paper yet?" she asked Dave. "No," Dave said. "You've got to see the paper," she said.

Dave later told me he was "blown away" to see the story featured on the front page with color photos, then see it jump to almost a full page inside.

A high-ranking editor later told me that the story had received the most page views or unique visitors—whatever that metric is called—in the 20+ year history of the online *Enquirer*, second-only to a story/photo of George W. Bush hugging Ashley Faulkner (in Lebanon, Ohio, in May, 2004), who had lost her mother in 9/11. And that, obviously, was a national story.

Ted's story was a local one, well, at least at first.

It developed into a national story, thanks in large part to Todd Frazier, who hit a key home run eight months later—April 18, 2013—when ESPN was in town to do a story on Ted. I'm not going to say anything more about that here, because if you aren't familiar with the special evening, I'm not going to spoil it. Mike and Diane do a terrific job telling the story in these pages. Let's just say that home run had a lot to do with why Ted wound up being the subject of a much-heralded ESPN *E:60* profile, an network news segment and, yes, this book.

There hasn't been a single time in my dozen or so contacts with Ted and his family in the three years since his story ran that I haven't been floored, laughed or marveled at what Ted's being invited to do next.

The best, of course, was an invitation from then Speaker of the House John Boehner to President Obama's State of the Union address on Feb. 13, 2013.

In my 40 years at the *Enquirer*, I've never been a personal witness to any more prestigious an event. It also helped me see a different side of Ted, a side I had always wanted to capture to help round out his portrait.

This book takes all that to the next level, the first narrative of which I'm aware that takes one inside the head of a person with Down syndrome and puts those thoughts into his or her own voice.

I didn't even realize until I began working on this foreword that Bronson Arroyo had pitched the night when Ted first served as batboy—August 17, 2012—and I'd forgotten that Frazier had hit a home run that night, too.

Hard to believe that more than three years has passed, but not hard at all to believe that Ted has come so far and done so much.

He's that kind o' guy.

—John Erardi, Crescent Springs, Kentucky

Prologue

FATHER SHAPPELLE SAID ONE DAY IN RELIGION CLASS THAT GOD adds a little something extra to everyone He makes. That's how He tells us apart. My something extra is a chromosome; I was born with Down syndrome. Some people might think that would make me sad, but it doesn't. I have a wonderful family and lots of friends who make me so very happy. They say to me, "You can do anything you set your mind to, Teddy." I really love my life.

I was christened Theodore Edwin Kremer, but my friends call me Teddy.

Today is my birthday, and it's really cold outside. My parents and I are going to The Back Porch Salon on Mulhauser Road to have my favorite meal—Mexican pizza! Whenever I go somewhere with my mom and dad, I always sit in the far back seats of our SUV. Not in the middle seats, like my brother does sometimes, but in the way, far back. My mom and dad always sit in the front and we talk about all kinds of things. Most of all, we talk about our family, our good friends, our church, and, of course, the Cincinnati Reds. I really like to look out the window and watch the trees go by. Today there is snow on the trees. The snow is very light, and I can see the dark tree limbs sticking out through the snowflakes.

Some of the snow has turned to ice, and the way it hangs off the branches reminds me of the cobwebs in our garage. Sister Martha, my preschool teacher, told me one time, "You know, Teddy, no two snowflakes are just alike. Every one is special." Then she patted me on the head. "And no two people are just alike. Every one of us is special. Don't you ever forget that." I haven't forgotten her words, not for a minute. I do think everybody is special in his own way.

I really like to watch sports on television, especially baseball, football and re-runs of the Wide World of Wrestling. Why do the coaches and players get so angry at the refs and umpires? They are just doing their jobs. When I was batboy for the Reds, I really liked getting to know the umps. They were really nice. I never get angry over the umps, but I do cry if my favorite team loses. I also might cry if someone makes fun of me because I have Down syndrome. I cried a lot when I was little, but now, instead of crying, I just walk away from mean people. Sometimes I feel sad. But I'm not sad for long, because most of the time I love my life.

I have had so many incredible adventures. Did you know I have flown on an airplane about twenty-five times and even sat in the cockpit once? And I've been to Disney World at least six times! The first time I saw Mickey I went crazy. Not only that, but also I was on the swim team for the Special Olympics, and last summer I was invited to the Daytona Firecracker 400. There was even a racecar at the Indianapolis Brickyard 500 with my name on it.

Two years ago, Speaker John Boehner invited me to hear President Obama's State of the Union Address. He even gave me a red baseball bat when I was in Washington, D.C. And guess what! While I was in the audience, President Obama waved at me. At me! I'm just an ordinary guy with Down syndrome. I mean that's crazy. Tony Bennett sat right behind me, and he didn't get a wave from the President. I bet that President Obama would be proud to know that when I visited the National Archives, I knew who had signed and who had not signed the Declaration of Independence. I also told the curator that the White House used to be called the Executive Mansion. She asked me how I knew that, and I told her, "Well, I listened when Sister Aloyse told us about it at Mercy!" Some things I can remember very well, and history is one of them. But can you believe the President waved at me? That was so cool.

And when I was in high school at Colerain High, I helped coach our team to the state championship. I still have the program from that game. It has the autographs of all the football players.

Yet nothing, not the state championship, Disney World, President Obama waving at me, or getting my own baseball card, can top the night of April 18, 2013. On that night, I was at the Great American Ball Park as batboy for the Cincinnati Reds. It was the second time I was the Reds batboy. The year before I was an honorary batboy for the Reds because my parents won a bid at a silent auction. When I walked on the field in that first game and met the players, it was so exciting! That night the Reds hit seven home runs and Manager Dusty Baker said, "Seems you're our good luck charm, Teddy." I guess that's why they invited me back.

My first time as batboy made me so happy, but the second time was beyond awesome. Before the game that night, I fist-bumped manager Dusty Baker, and then high-fived Brandon Philips and Jay Bruce. "Hey, Teddy!" Chris Heisey and Bronson Arroyo yelled at me. The players knew me from the first time, so I was in a great mood and I couldn't stop smiling. I don't know if you pay attention to the Reds games, but if the pitchers strike out at least 11 batters in a game, all the fans get a free La Rosa's pizza. If you know me at all, you know I love La Rosa's! I would eat it for breakfast if Mom would let me. I kept my fingers crossed and watched as the Reds struck out one batter after another.

Being a batboy is more than watching the game and wishing for strikeouts. It's a lot of hard work. All those steps up and out of the dugout picking up bats and taking balls to the umpire is exhausting, but I love it! You get to meet the players and have the best seat at the game. The first five innings were exciting but in the sixth inning, something wonderful happened.

I was standing near the dugout, smiling and cutting up with some of the players, when I noticed that Todd Frazier, my favorite player, was on deck. Back in the second inning Todd struck out.

When he came back to the dugout, I said, "That's okay, Todd. You'll do better next time." We were beating the Marlins 9-1 and Joey Votto was on base. "Hey, Todd," I said above the crowd noise. He looked over at me and I told him, "I love you, man."

He smiled and replied, "I love you too, Teddy."

I smiled back and said, "Hit a home run for me."

He nodded, "You got it."

As Todd walked up to home plate, his theme song "Fly Me to the Moon" played on the speakers. He got up to bat and on the first pitch, he swung and missed. He stepped out, looked at the third base coach and then got ready again. "You can do it, Todd!" I yelled. The pitcher threw the pitch and Todd swung hard. I can still hear the sound of the ball hitting the bat. It was a loud crack. The ball looked like one of those bottle rockets we shoot on July 4. The crowd started cheering as Todd ran to first. The ball was high and flying way back. I could tell it was going to be a long home run to center field. I started jumping up and down in the dugout. When the ball landed over the fence, everyone went crazy.

Jay Bruce yelled to me, "Go up to home plate!" I ran out of the dugout and was at home before Todd got to second base. He rounded third and saw me standing at home with my arms in the air. Todd grinned all the way to the plate. When Todd touched home and we high-fived, I don't think I could have been more excited. I was following Todd to the dugout when I heard someone call my name. I turned around and the umpire held out Todd's bat. I was so happy that I had forgotten to get his bat. And I'm the batboy! I ran and grabbed the bat, and then hurried back to the dugout. Todd saw me and held out his arms. I jumped up on him and gave him a big hug. I couldn't help it! My favorite player had just hit a home run for my favorite team, the Cincinnati Reds. And he did it for me! I bet when I was little, Mom and Dad would've never thought this would happen to their son. The Reds won the game against the Marlins, and Dusty Baker told me, "You know what, Teddy, maybe you really are our good luck charm." To remind me of that night, he gave me a black sweatband like the players wear. And guess what— Chapman struck out the side in the top of the ninth and we all got free pizza! Did I tell you I love my life?

Chapter 1

FOR CHRISTMAS THIS YEAR, SANTA CLAUS BROUGHT ME AN IPAD. My brother, David, said I should write about my life as a person with Down syndrome. He's very proud of all that I have accomplished in my life. He gets very upset when people say I have a disability. He thinks "disability" is a stupid word. (I'm not allowed to call people or animals stupid, just things or words.) I guess I don't see myself as a person with a dis-ability either. I am just a regular person who happens to have Down syndrome.

David remembers hearing my parents talk about me after they brought me home from the hospital. He was only five, but he really wanted to help me. So, one night he was watching television and a commercial came on with the actor who played Trapper John on *Mash*. In the commercial, the actor said, "To learn more about Down syndrome, contact the National Down Syndrome Congress." My brother then raced over to my mom and dad and said, "We need to contact them, because isn't that what Teddy has?" My mom and dad were really surprised, because I was only a few weeks old, and they hadn't told David yet that I had Down syndrome.

My brother and I are really good friends. We talk on the phone almost every day, and I try to visit him and my nephews at least once a month. For my birthday this year, he is driving down from South Bend with his wife and my two nephews, who are eight and five. I'm so pumped to have cake and ice cream with Trey and Cord. Last summer David and I took them to the Reds game and I gave them a first-game certificate. Because my dad and I work part time for the Reds, we were able to get them seats right behind the Reds' bench. That was so awesome! Trey and Cord kept waving to all the players! Little kids are so much fun. They get excited about everything! I get excited about everything too, especially the Cincinnati Reds.

My mom told me one day, "Teddy, you make me feel young and old at the same time." I think that's because she enjoys all the things I do, but at the same time, she gets tired following me around. Then she told me, "You have the energy of a five-year-old. At Disney World." That's a good thing, I think.

January 8, 1983 is my birthday. Every time I have a birthday, I ask my mother, "Can you tell me about the day I was born?" Mom always tells me the same story, but I never get tired of hearing it.

"You were a very special baby, not because you had Down syndrome, but because you were always smiling. I knew as soon as I saw you, I would hold you in my heart forever." A few days after I was born, the geneticist on call that day said I would be better off in an institution.

"Cheryl and Dave," the doctor said, "I have some very grim news." She paused and glanced at my chart. "Theodore won't be able to interact with people, use the bathroom, and maybe not even walk. He will have limited communication skills and will probably never smile. I am so sorry, but I think it's important for you to hear the truth." Mom and Dad couldn't believe what they were hearing. The doctor continued, "He will never spell or do math, and his IQ will be somewhere between 20 and 40." Mom says that is really low. Then the doctor said something not very nice. "With his lack of muscle strength, playing sports is out of the question. But, most of all, he will never have many friends, so I really think he should be placed in an institution. He'll be better off there, and you can visit him as much as you want."

Mom and Dad said at first their feelings were hurt, but then they got really mad. They looked the doctor in the eye, and Dad said, "We don't believe any of that." My mom asked, "Why would we want to hide our child from the world? We're both educators. We want to know what to do for Teddy right now!"

Stunned by my parents' reactions, the doctor said, "Oh, I didn't know that I was talking to people with an education. Now if you lived in the ghetto, you would just take your baby home and never know anything was wrong with him."

My mom had an African-American roommate in the hospital at the time, and she was so angry at that comment she couldn't even speak. Once the doctor walked out of the room, my mom refused to see her again.

Every time Mom tells me the story, I raise my hands and shout, "No sports, no friends?! What does that doctor know?" Then I dance around the kitchen. She was sort of right about math though.

IT WAS A VERY HARD TIME for my parents back then, especially since they were so young. They felt like they had nowhere to turn. Luckily, Dad had his best friend Doug Daugherty to lean on, and besides Dad, my mom had her best friend Joan Geisen for added support. My grandparents helped them as much as they could, but they didn't know much about Down syndrome. My aunts and uncles and the rest of my mom and dad's friends really loved me and wanted to help, but they didn't know what to do either. All I know is that it takes a village to figure things out. Everyone thinks doctors are always right, so it was a very confusing time for everybody.

Lucky for me, my parents listened to our pediatrician, Ron Levin. He was mad when my parents told him what the doctor in the hospital said about me and other special needs children. "She didn't know she was talking to a couple of stubborn, bright, young teachers," Ron said. "I am so glad you didn't listen to her. "Ron brought in his own geneticist, who told my parents to get me started in therapy as soon as possible. Ron recommended that my parents send me to Mercy Montessori for preschool. His own children attended school there, and he knew they accepted a certain number of special needs children every year.

So now I had at least one doctor who believed in me. He saw me as a real person who would someday dream and play and maybe even make a difference in the world. I was more than just a Down syndrome baby. I was Teddy. One day, after my mom told me this story, I got on my iPad and read that one in every 691 babies in the United States is born with Down syndrome. That's 6,000 special babies like me every year. I wonder how many of them had parents who believed they could fly to the moon if they wanted to? I wonder how many Down syndrome babies have been sent away to institutions? I read online about a place in Columbus, Ohio, called The Orient. It's now a prison, but back when I was a baby, it was an institution for special needs people, as well as the insane. It looked so sad. Some of the patients were strapped to their beds, some were chained to the walls, and others were wrapped in tight white blankets. They looked like they could hardly breathe. They didn't look like they went to school or therapy. I don't think anyone really cared about them, not even their parents.

I HAVE LOTS OF FRIENDS LIKE me, and they all have supportive parents. Most of them live at home, though some of my friends live in small apartments or group homes. A couple in my dance class got married last year, and the two of them live in a small house on the bus line. Some of my favorite friends with Down syndrome take ballroom dancing with me on Wednesday nights. There's one girl I really like, though she's older than me. I always try to be her partner though I like everyone in my class.

My mother said "flying to the moon" is just an expression. It reminds me of the scene in *Wicked* when the witch flies up into the air on her broom. As she flies above the stage, the song she sings is "Defying Gravity". I really love that song. When we're in the car I might sing, "I'm through accepting limits 'cause someone says they're so! Some things I cannot change, but till I try, I'll never know!" I think I have a great voice, but my mom, dad, and brother don't agree. Dad tells me, "You can only sing when it's warm enough to roll down the windows." My dad thinks he's funny.

In that play, the wicked witch is not evil like everyone thinks. Elphaba just sees life in a different way. And she is green. So everyone is afraid of her because she looks different. Sometimes people are afraid of me because I look different. Most people accept me the way I am, but sometimes people ignore me or look away when I try to talk to them. A few kids in school would say mean things. My mom says people are afraid of what they don't understand. Like Elphaba. But her green color isn't going to hold her back! Then Elphaba sings the song I love and flies away! She is so cool.

When Mom knew I was going to tell my story, she said, "You know, Teddy, you have to tell everything. The good times and the not-so-good times." I thought that was okay. Mostly, I am happy and I love all of my friends. Sometimes I feel sad, but I try not to let it show. The words I say are shorter than how I think. Like, I really miss my older brother, David; Erin; and my two nephews. When I talk to them on my cell phone, I say, "I miss you," but my feelings for them are a lot bigger than my words. I show how I feel about people in lots of ways. I give hugs and high-fives. I smile and shake hands all the time. Sometimes people ignore me when I wave, or school kids laugh and make fun of me. That really doesn't bother me. It did but I'm kind of used to it by now. Besides, I have a lot of friends who love me. My mom says there are many people who only have one or two friends, or none at all, like those people who were in the Orient Institution. So I'm very lucky, yet I still don't understand why people are mean. It's too easy to be nice, and it's way more fun.

I remember one day in high school this kid pushed me into the lockers. It's not like he made me cry or anything. I just walked away. Mom told me later, "I'm proud of you. It gives you more power than staying there and fighting." Mom is smart when it comes to what is best for me.

I know I said I love my life. I do. Even the sad parts don't get me down. Sister Aloyse told me one time, "God gave you the gift of joy, Teddy." That's a great gift to have because I can smile through my tears if I need to.

Chapter 2

I AM SO HAPPY MY PARENTS DIDN'T PUT ME IN AN INSTITUTION. I never would've been batboy for the Reds or gotten to eat at La Rosa's or even gone to school with regular kids. I'm glad my parents told the doctor, "NO WAY! Teddy is staying with his family! We're going to take him home and love him just like our other son." She said the "special home" didn't have any expectations for kids with Down syndrome. I don't know why, because I have friends with Down syndrome that do lots of things. My mom says it was different thirty years ago. The doctors didn't know as much about Down syndrome as they do now. That's why some doctors didn't expect much from people like me. I asked my mom one time if I had a disease. She said, "No, people with Down syndrome don't have a disease. They just have an extra chromosome." My mom said it took years for people to figure it out. That's why so many people with Down syndrome were treated unfairly and died so young. Years ago children with Down syndrome would catch the flu or a virus, and they would become dehydrated. The dehydration would actually cause the children to die because doctors didn't know that children with Down syndrome needed extra electrolytes. Down syndrome children often lose lots of electrolytes soon after becoming sick to their stomachs. This often causes children with Down syndrome to be confused and even hospitalized. Luckily, not many die from this anymore.

A few nights ago I went upstairs to say goodnight to my parents.

Mom was sitting on the couch with a book on her lap, and she was crying. "What's wrong, Mom?" I asked. "Why are you so sad?"

"Oh, Teddy, it's this book. I know it's fiction, but it's based on things that used to happen all the time years ago."

"Like what?" I asked her.

"Sometimes after a mother had a baby, doctors would take the baby away and tell the parents the baby was dead. But he really wasn't, he was just made a little different. Then the nurses would put the baby in a place where he would never know his family. And his mother would never know that she had this very special son." My mother then put her arms around me and told me she loved me very much. I said, "I love you too, Mom. So, you see? You shouldn't be sad. You didn't lose me."

My mom and dad read all the time; that's probably because they used to be teachers. My mom taught 4th, 5th, and 6th grades at Struble Elementary School for seven years before David and I were born. Once I started full time kindergarten at Mercy Montessori, she went back to teaching and taught 2nd grade.

Now, my mom is the curriculum specialist for the Northwest School District. She hopes to retire next year. Even though she can't wait, I know she will miss all her teaching friends. My dad is already retired. Before he became assistant principal at Colerain High School, he was assistant principal at several middle schools. Before he became an assistant principal at any school, he taught Drafting and Driver's Ed. He said teaching teens how to drive was much harder than being an assistant principal. I have never been interested in driving anything but golf carts.

When Dad took students out in the Driver's Ed car, it usually went pretty well. Not always though. One time he came home and even before he took off his coat, we could smell smoke. Mom asked him, "What have you been doing? Burning leaves? You smell awful." Even though it was cold, she walked over to the windows and opened one up.

Dad rolled his eyes. "Just another day driving kids around."

We could tell there was more to his story. Mom said, "Something happen?"

Then he told us about his crazy day. He had taken four students out to show them how to drive. It was early in the year so it was only their second lesson. "I waited till they got out of school and we all piled into the car," Dad said. "I don't let them wear coats while driving, so I had them put all their coats and book bags in the trunk."

"You always do that, don't you?" Mom asked.

"Every time. So we were going down the street—I was in the passenger seat and Linda was driving. We were practicing stop and go, stop and go. Well, we went by a construction site and I smelled something funny."

"What did you think it was?" I asked.

"Actually, I thought a big tractor trailer was blowing smoke and didn't think anything of it."

"A truck was on fire?" I asked.

"No, just wait." Dad shook his head and kept going. "So, I got to thinking it would be a good time to show the kids what to do if they thought it was their own car making a smell. So we stopped in the parking lot across from La Rosa's."

"Oh, man, La Rosa's was on fire?" I said. I sure hoped that wasn't the case because I love their pizza.

"No, La Rosa's wasn't on fire. So, anyway we lifted up the hood and I was showing them how to check the oil and brake fluid. I still smelled something but didn't pay much attention because there were trucks going by." Dad sat down at the kitchen counter. "Then I took them around back to show them where the spare tire is, and when I opened the trunk it was full of smoke."

"No!" Mom said.

"Oh, yeah. When the air hit the smoke, it flamed up. One of the jackets was on fire. A girl screamed. It was nuts. Flames were everywhere. I dragged out the jacket and threw it on the ground. "

My eyes were wide. "Wow! A fire in the trunk!"

"It could've blown up the gas tank!" Mom said.

"I know," Dad said. "I thought of that. It turns out one of the kids left a lit cigarette in his jacket pocket. It took me a while to get the truth out of him. He hemmed and hawed and finally admitted he had been smoking before I picked them up. He said a teacher came around the corner and instead of putting his cigarette out, he wrapped his hand around the cigarette."

"Palming," Mom said.

Dad looked at her. "How do you know that?"

Mom smiled and shrugged. "I know things. Go on."

"Anyway, he thought it was out and instead of throwing it away, he put it in his pocket. His pocket of all things! Who does that?"

"He does," I said. "Wow, he almost burned up the car."

"And us with it. When we got back to school I took him to the office. I think he got suspended."

Dad walked to the fridge and got a Coke. "I need this."

"Well, I guess your students learned a lot today," Mom told him.

"We all learned something," Dad said before he sipped his soda.

It was a crazy story and I thought Dad acted pretty cool. I don't know what I would've done. I know one thing—I'll never put something already on fire in my pocket! But I will never smoke so I guess I won't have to worry about that.

Chapter 3

MY DAD WAS A GOOD TEACHER AND HE LOVED WORKING WITH kids, even if they tried to burn up his Driver's Ed car. Both my parents loved teaching, but they loved teaching me the most. But like I said before, they had high expectations for me. And it started soon after I was born. Mom and Dad told me lots about when I was a baby. I remember clapping my hands while I looked at myself in the mirror, but that's about all I remember from those years. Everything else I had to ask Mom.

Mom said I began physical therapy in Ron's office when I was two weeks old. Dr. Ron said my muscles were weak and he was worried my legs might become floppy. He also told mom I had a weak tongue and weak cheek muscles. That made it difficult for Mom to feed me. The therapist showed my mother how to position me so I would learn to take a bottle easier. Later on, the therapist would make me roll on this big orange ball with my arms out. "You hated that orange ball. You would cry as soon as you saw it," Mom told me.

When I was five weeks old, Mom started taking me to infant stimulation classes. My classes sure had some big names! She took me every other day for several hours until I was three. According to my mom, my teachers showed me colors and shapes. They taught me to clap my hands to music as I looked into a mirror. The teachers also encouraged me to look up, so I would strengthen my neck. They taught me to balance better. I had a hard time figuring out that there were things to the left and right side of body. My mom said until I learned that, I would only reach my hands forward because I didn't understand how to cross the middle of my body.

At my three month check-up, my pediatrician told Mom it was important for me to build my arm and leg muscles so I could learn to roll over and crawl. Mom still didn't think I was holding my head up very well, so she put me in water therapy at the YMCA. Every time I went into the water, I pulled my head up because I didn't like having all that water in my eyes. Who would? It helped my neck grow stronger and soon I could hold my head up like other babies my age. She took me swimming several times a week until I was three.

The other moms did not want me in the water with their children, so my mom had to put me in a class all by myself. "They would look at you and take their babies out of the pool," my grandmother told me. "That hurt your mom's feelings and made her mad at the same time." Maybe they were afraid I might get hurt. At least that's what my grandmother says. Eventually, I became a good swimmer and I was put in classes with other kids. When I was three, I took swimming lessons with all my classmates at Mercy Montessori.

Besides swimming, Mom took me on outings and family events. My teachers told her to take me out as much as possible. They said, "Children with Down syndrome copy what they see, and if they don't see what's right, they aren't going to progress."

WHEN I WAS ELEVEN MONTHS OLD, Mom took me to a private speech class two mornings a week. My teacher, Tina Veale, helped me to say my words. For many people with Down syndrome, our tongues are too large for our mouths. She used to flick my tongue to make sure I kept it in my mouth. Tina also helped me with my eating. People with Down syndrome like foods that are smooth and soft. Mashed potatoes are still one of my favorites. And Mexican food. I can eat refried beans and burritos all day long. Eventually I started eating regular kid food, like hot dogs and macaroni and cheese. Mom and Dad wanted me to try all kinds of food, but I was very stubborn. Then one day, I guess I was about ten or eleven, I tried pizza. I loved it! Now I eat pizza at La Rosa's all the time. But no matter what I had to eat, I always had to go to speech class. I worked with Tina twice a week until I was 18. I also took speech from another teacher at Mercy Montessori. My Mom said, "We didn't want to leave any stone unturned." I asked her what turning over rocks had to do with all my therapy classes. She told me, "That just means we wanted to make sure we tried everything to help you, Teddy." I wasn't always happy about my speech classes, but I'm glad my mother made me go.

It's funny how I dreaded speech class, but now I have no problem getting up in front of people and giving speeches. I love talking to people, though sometimes my mom and dad think I talk too much. Mom always reminds me not to interrupt when other people are speaking. She says, "It is just as important to listen as it is to talk." But I really love to talk! The world is so full of exciting things that I can't help myself sometimes. I wonder if my mom had any idea how much those speech classes would help? My mom and dad made a lot of sacrifices for me, and for my brother. My mom says it's easy to make sacrifices for people you love.

By the time I was two, my muscles grew strong enough for mom to start doing what she calls "fine motor therapy" with me. First, I would try to pick up cotton balls with tongs. Then she had me pick up straight pins with tweezers. That's hard! I learned to color with crayons and then paints and pencils. Finally, I learned how to cut with plastic scissors.

By the time I entered preschool at Mercy, my fine motor skills were much better. It did, however, take several years of therapy for me to learn to print. But I finally caught on. I still can't do cursive though. I really try. When I sign my name or write something on paper, I have to print. I love signing my name so it looks like cursive. I do this by printing the letters as close together as I can. Since I got my iPad, I type most of my notes and ideas on that. It sure makes my writing go faster, though I still struggle sometimes.

I know it was tough on my parents when my brother and I were little. Mom gave up her job at Struble to take care of us. The only money coming in was Dad's pay as a drafting teacher. Eventually, he made extra money by teaching driver's education classes after school, but it was still hard for them. Even though Mom tutored kids some, the bills piled up every week and my parents sometimes had to ask my grandparents for help.

David got to play all kinds of sports after school while I was in therapy. I bet he had more fun than I did. He has always been good at sports, especially baseball and basketball. He's still great at sports—you should see him when he plays golf. He can hit the ball a mile! And he's really smart. Even though I love my life, sometimes I wish I could be as smart as my big brother.

Whenever I compare myself to David, Mom tells me to be happy for all that I've accomplished. "We all have unique gifts," she tells me. "Your best gifts are your joyfulness and your willingness to learn." In school, I seldom gave up, even though some things took longer for me to learn than other kids my age. But once I learn something, I never forget it. I guess that's better than being a fast learner and forgetting everything. Ha! That's a joke. I would rather be a fast learner and remember everything. Then I'd be like Stephen Hawking, the man in the wheelchair who talks about space. But like Mom says, I shouldn't complain, because I do have an excellent memory—one of my special gifts. She also says I can learn just about anything—well, maybe not hard math stuff, like Stephen Hawking does—even though it just takes me a little longer. If I could learn the hard math, I would want to be an astronaut. It would be so cool to be the first special needs person in space. Just like Todd Frazier's song says, "Fly Me to the Moon!"

Chapter 4

MOM TOOK DR. RON'S ADVICE AND PUT ME ON THE WAITING LIST at Mercy Montessori when I was only a month old. Mom had learned that ten percent of the student body at Mercy was made up of special needs children like me. Mom also thought I would get a better education there because I would be treated as a normal child. In the public schools, I would be placed in a special education resource room. At that time, Mercy Montessori was the only school in the city that placed special needs children in the same classroom as the typical kids.

Right after I turned two, Sister Jacintha, the principal of Mercy, called my mom and asked that she bring me in for an interview. Mom said, "I was so excited to see you in that little gray Eton suit with the Peter Pan collar. That gray captain's hat and gray winter coat made you look so cute." I suppose I made quite an impression, because Sister Jacintha and Sister Martha talked about that little gray suit for years.

The first person I met there was Sister Jacintha, and I liked her from the start.

Even though I learned many things from my teachers and liked them a lot, I really loved my principal. When she would visit my preschool and first grade classrooms, she would pick me up and sit me on her lap. She hugged me all the time. I always felt love coming from her. I know she was proud of me.

Years later, I came home from high school and Mom met me at the door.

"Teddy, we need to talk for a minute."

I knew it was something serious. I tried to remember if I had done something wrong at school.

Mom was sad, and she told me, "Sister Jacintha is very sick."

"Does she have the flu again?"

"No, Teddy, sicker than that." Mom always told me the truth, but I could tell this was hard for her. "She has colon cancer."

I remember a friend's dad who died from cancer, and I was instantly very sad. I didn't know what to say at first. Then I asked, "Can she get better?"

Mom shook her head and gave me a hug. I cried on her shoulder. Sister Jacintha died a few weeks later. The day she died Mom told me, "One of her final wishes was that you be a pallbearer for her." That made me really cry. I miss her very much. I still feel her love for me.

IT WAS SISTER JACINTHA WHO WALKED me down to Sister Martha's classroom for my interview. Sister Martha was the preschool and kindergarten teacher. Because my mom and Sister Jacintha had talked so much about Sister Martha, the minute we entered her classroom, I said, "Sister Martha!" She smiled and then knelt down in front of me. She looked me straight in the eyes and said, "Hi, Teddy. I can tell you are going to be a great student." Then I started giggling at a rabbit running under the classroom tables. "Oh dear," Sister Martha said. "I guess we forgot to put Rudy on his leash." She looked at my mom. "It's so hectic at the end of the day, especially with all the snow and the galoshes and mittens we have to put on." Sister Martha looked around the room until she found the leash and attached it to the rabbit's collar. She held the rabbit out to me. "Meet Rudy," she said. "Would you like to hold his leash?" At least that's the story Mom tells. I don't remember the words, but I do remember Rudy the Rabbit.

MOM SAYS SISTER MARTHA AND I really hit it off that day. She's the one who suggested that I come in for tutoring sessions two days a week. From January until September, before I even started preschool, Sister Martha "readied" me for Mercy. Mom calls it "acclimation." Another big word! Because my tutoring was from 3:00 to 5:00 in the afternoon, David had to go to Latch Key. We both had really long days. We had no time for video games or television with all the school and sports and tutoring sessions.

The next year at Mercy I was supposed to start half-day preschool. Sister Jacintha told Mom, "You do realize that all our preschool children are potty-trained?" Mom and Sister Martha told her that I would be ready by the time school started. Here go Mom and Sister Martha again, setting high goals for me. But they won. I was potty trained by the time I was three, and seldom had an accident. Even at night. Some people say that's amazing. Well, they don't know my mom or Sister Martha. Mom said there was a boy with Down syndrome at her school who is seven, and he is still not potty trained. That would never happen around my house. Not with my mom. She would have had that child potty trained really fast.

Sister Martha was strict like Mom. "Teddy, you've interrupted Matthew again!" she said one time. "Let him finish his story. Then you can talk." Sister told the class that listening is just as important as talking. But listening is hard for me because I love talking to people. I guess that comes from all the speech classes my mom made me take over the years. She wanted me to talk, so I talk!

Sister Martha was tough on me, but I loved being in her class. She always had pets, not just Rudy the Rabbit, but ferrets, hamsters, gerbils, white mice, and even several rats. It was because of those rats that I met my first preschool friend, Lauren Roedersheimer. She loved the rats and would hold them in her lap and pet them. I was scared to touch them at first, but Lauren told me not to be afraid. Finally, she put one of the baby rats in my lap and said, "See? He's really nice, just like you." Lauren and I became great friends over the years, but she got ahead of me in school. I had to stay back a few grades, but then I met her sister Renee. Renee was three years younger than Lauren. We were good friends all through Mercy and even in high school. Renee and I even went to prom together! I'll tell you about that later.

My dad always asked about my friends at school, even when I was in preschool. When I told my dad about Lauren and the rats, he said, "Rats! Your teacher has rats in her room?"

"Yeah, they are so cool," I told him.

Dad shook his head. "Rats are not cool. Does she have pet roaches, too?"

I laughed at that. "No way!"

Dad could've been right. If she had had more space, who knows what would've been running around her room. "Rats are really wonderful, smart animals," Sister Martha told us. "They are just terribly misunderstood. Like many things." Sister Martha let all her students take turns holding her pets. "Please be gentle with them," she would say as we held the rats and ferrets. I was always careful. I was so afraid I might hurt them!

We didn't just play with animals; we also practiced many things that would help us take of ourselves. We learned to wash and hang clothes, stack cylinder blocks, manipulate beads and letters, polish silver, count coins, and put sounds to letters. One day Sister Martha said, "Guess what we're having for lunch."

"Peanut butter and jelly!"

"Sloppy Joes!"

One kid even said, "Skyline chili!"

We were all wrong.

"Today, we are making our lunch. The very delicious stone soup."

"I can't eat rocks," I told her. "Can we have pizza?"

Stone soup is made with real stones, but you don't really eat them. You eat everything else in the pot. You first boil several rocks in a pot of water, and then each student puts a vegetable they brought from home into the pot. We let the vegetables cook while Sister Martha read us a story about a poor couple that cooked stones in a pot of water over an open fire. The people of the village became curious and began adding vegetables and spices to the pot. Then the poor couple shared the soup with the entire village and everybody had enough to eat. I loved stone soup day, and always ate a bowlful. The story was good, too.

Sister Martha also made us keep a change of clothes in a shoebox, just in case we spilled something on our clothes or had a potty accident. She didn't make a big deal out of it if we messed up our clothes. She simply told us to change in the bathroom and put the old clothes in the shoebox to take home. To this day, I tell everyone, "Sister Martha is the best teacher I have ever had!"

In my first years at Mercy, I would sometimes miss school because I had ear infections. This usually meant a trip to the doctor's office and more tubes in my ears. When I would go back to school, Sister Martha would say, "I missed you, Teddy. But now you have lessons to make up." I was more upset about the extra lessons I had to do than the tubes the doctor put in my ears.

Sometimes I would not feel like working with beads or sandpaper letters. Sister Martha never cut me any slack, and sometimes I would get mad at her. "No," I told her. "I don't want to do work anymore; I'm too tired."

She would look at me and say, "You're not getting away with this, Teddy Kremer. It would be easy to give in and let you zone out, but I care about you too much." She sometimes would read quotes to inspire me, or to make me feel guilty. One day when I was upset, she said, "Thomas Carlyle wrote, 'If you go as far as you can see, then you can go further.' That's what I want for you Teddy—to go further than people expect you to go. Besides, the work I ask you to do is very important. If you stop practicing, you'll have to start all over again."

I asked her if Mr. Carlyle had to do "twice as many lessons" when he missed school. She laughed and said, "Probably so." Then she would tell one of her silly jokes and get me laughing. I couldn't stay mad at her for very long.

I remember a pink tower that I had to take apart and put back together. The tower was made of different sized cubes. Sister Martha showed me how to build it, placing the largest cube on the bottom, then the next largest, and so forth, until we had used up all of the cubes. As Sister built the tower, she would ask me questions. "How much smaller is this cube than the one on the bottom of the tower?" At first I would show her by using my fingers. Later on, I learned to say things like "half the size," or "a fourth of the size." After we built the tower and talked about it, Sister Martha would knock it down and tell me to build it again. The first time she did that, I couldn't believe it. By the tenth time, I knew what was coming.

"Why do I have to keep doing this?" I asked Sister Martha.

"Because every time you build it, you learn something new. Isn't that what life is about?" She had an answer for everything. That tower really drove me crazy. At first, it was hard to figure out what block came next. But I eventually conquered that pink tower. By the time I was in first grade, I could build the tower in no time. Years later, Sister Martha told me that sometimes I might be slower, but I always ended up learning the lesson. At my twenty-first birthday party, she gave me a big hug and said, "Teddy, you still haven't reached a plateau. And I don't think you ever will." I asked my mom what she meant by "plateau," and my mom said it meant a stopping point in your learning. Sister Martha is right; I will never stop learning, no matter how much extra time I need.

SISTER MARTHA NOW LIVES IN LOUISVILLE at the Lake Saint Joseph Retreat Center with her German shepherd, Heidi. She manages the Center and coordinates the food and activities for the retreats.

In late 2014, Mom told me, "Teddy, Sister Martha called and wanted to know when you were coming for a visit."

"Let's go tomorrow!" I said.

"Well, we can go this weekend. How about that?"

I raised my arms and said, "Yes!" I love going to see my favorite teacher. She is always so happy to see me.

We left early the next Saturday morning. I was excited the whole way down to Louisville. As soon as we got there, I jumped out of the car and knocked on the front door.

"Sister Martha! It's me!" I yelled.

"Teddy! Oh, Teddy," she said as she gave me a big hug. "I have missed you so much."

We sat in her living room and talked about all kinds of stuff. Mostly we talked about my school days at Montessori and my days with the Reds. "You were one of my favorite students. Some days you would sit on my lap and give me the biggest hugs while I rocked you. You were always smiling," Sister Martha said. "But you sure didn't like to make decisions. You always wanted me to pick the activity, the color of paper, or the lunchtime drink for you." She laughed. "I never would because I wanted you to learn to choose for yourself, not just in school, but in all parts of life. Montessori is all about 'on-the-job training,' isn't that right, Teddy?" I agreed with her now, but I wasn't too sure back in school.

Even though there were times I would get mad at Sister Martha, I do appreciate all I learned from her. She has always been like a second mom to me, and I guess I was her special child.

Before we left she told me, "I sure am proud of you, Teddy. When I am talking to my friends here, I always tell them about my famous student." She then gave me another big hug. I did not want to leave Sister Martha that day. I started to cry as I walked with Mom and Dad to the car. Sister Martha waved goodbye from her front porch, and Mom said Sister Martha was crying, too. "Can we come back and visit her again?" I asked Mom.

"Sure, Teddy, we can do that," she said. "Let's make sure we don't wait so long between visits, though."

One of my best friends in Sister Martha's class and all through Mercy Montessori was Matt Moore. I recently sent him an e-mail telling him about my visit to Sister Martha. He wrote back and said he was very jealous because Sister Martha was one of his favorite teachers. I remember Sister Martha used to tap Matt on the head and ask, "Is anyone at home?" He was a skinny kid, and he used to zone out in class like I did sometimes. We both struggled with math, and maybe that's why we became such good friends.

Matt now lives in Tokyo, but we're still very good friends. I see him whenever he is in Cincinnati visiting his family. He went to Xavier University and majored in advertising because, he said, the guy sitting next to him at orientation was majoring in advertising, and there were no math classes in that major. After graduating from Xavier, he attended an advertising school in Atlanta. While there, he met a man who wrote the line, "Just Do It!" This person really liked Matt's work and ideas, so he hired him to work at his agency. He then sent Matt to Japan to work at Nike. Matt is very successful and loves his job. I know Sister Martha and all of his teachers at Mercy are very proud of him. I am.

Chapter 5

DURING PRESCHOOL I REALLY STARTED GETTING INTO SPORTS. Mercy has an inside swimming pool and every student has swim class at least once a week. Because of my swimming therapy when I was an infant, I already knew how to swim when I started at Mercy. By the time I was seven, I had made the Mercy swim team and was one of our best swimmers. I was into other sports, too. When I was four, I started playing lollipop soccer on a neighborhood team. I guess it's called "lollipop" because it's for little kids. My brother, David, told me, "You know, during practice you would kick the ball and then sit right down. I made you promise not to do that on game days. But guess what."

"What?" I thought I knew but wanted him to tell me.

"During the games, you wouldn't sit down," he said. "But you still didn't pay attention to what was going on. I would yell, 'Kick the ball, Teddy!' You didn't kick the ball once during a game. You were more interested in watching butterflies and picking dandelions."

I always loved those soccer games because our team would get snacks and sodas afterwards. The best games were when we had pizza! I was the only kid on the team with Down syndrome, but it didn't seem to matter to anyone. And I saw some cool butterflies.

Little League baseball was a different story. Some of the kids on the other teams made fun of me, and I cried. I guess it's okay to cry when you're six years old. I really didn't understand why the kids were so mean to me. During the school day, none of the kids at Mercy made fun of me, so why did the kids on the baseball team laugh at me? I couldn't understand what I was doing wrong. I told

Dad I wanted to quit, but he and Mom wouldn't let me. "If you start it, you finish it," Dad said. Now I'm glad he wouldn't let me quit. When my dad talked to Coach Tom about some of the kids on the other teams, Coach was really upset. He had no idea that some of the kids laughed at me. He put a stop to that right away, and I even made some good friends in the league.

My brother helped me with my game too, especially after that day when I came home crying.

My brother asked me, "Why don't I toss you some balls to hit in the back yard?"

I was so excited to practice with my brother. He was a great baseball player. My dad decided to practice with me, too. So almost every night that summer, my brother pitched balls to me and my dad helped me swing. After a while, I got to where I could hit the ball every time.

Practicing with my brother and dad really helped me become a team player. I tried really hard to hit the ball far enough to get on base. Sometimes I would even bunt. One day, I actually hit a ball that rolled between the outfielders. I ran like it was the World Series and when I touched home plate, I pumped my fists in the air. Mom and Dad and my brother cheered as loud for that home run as anything I have ever done. After that day, no one on any team made fun of me. I might be a kid with Down syndrome, but now I was a kid who could hit the ball and score runs. I learned a lot about baseball that year, but most of all I learned how much I loved the game. I looked forward to Little League every year that I was old enough to play.

I WAS SAD WHEN LITTLE LEAGUE was over that summer and I had to return to school. Though I was almost seven, I was still in kindergarten. Lauren had moved up to first grade, but I met her sister Renee and we became good friends. I still saw a lot of Lauren because our families were good friends, and we did a lot of fun things together outside of school. I really liked going over to the Roedersheimer's house, and they came to our house for dinner a lot. We sometimes had them come over on Christmas day.

The Christmas I was six something really wonderful happened to our family. It was early in the morning, and I had just opened most of my presents from Santa. I got a video game, some Disney movies, a train, and a drum set. Dad shook his head when I started banging on the drum. "I wonder who told Santa to bring him a drum set," Dad said.

Mom smiled and looked out the window. She said, "It's snowing!"

I ran to the window; the snow was the size of quarters. I love snow! It's so pretty and makes the world seem soft and nice. I think everyone is in a better mood when the first snow falls. But when people have to drive in it, they get grumpy.

I decided to open the front door and catch some snowflakes on my tongue.

"Teddy!" Mom yelled from the living room. "Put your coat on first!" But it was too late; I was already out the door. I started to catch a few snowflakes in my mouth, and then I heard a small cry. On the sidewalk in front of our house was a large brown dog. He was partially covered with snow and shivering. He looked really hungry.

I ran back into the house and yelled, "Mom, Dad! There's a dog on our sidewalk!" My parents came out and stood on our front porch. My brother, David, ran outside and started jumping up and down. "It's a Christmas present!" he hollered. Dad told us to not get too close. But when he saw how cold the dog was, he let him in the front door.

"Maybe he's got rabies," Mom said. Dad didn't think so. We gave him some of our meat loaf leftovers. He ate like he had not eaten for a week. I was a little scared of him because he was as big as me.

But then he looked at me with sad eyes, and I asked Mom, "Can we keep him?"

"Well, he might belong to someone."

"If he does, he's been gone for a while," Dad told us. "But he's still a puppy. A big puppy."

My brother asked, "Can we keep him? If he's not someone's?"

Dad looked at Mom and said, "We'll have to get him checked out."

Suddenly, we all noticed a terrible smell. "Phew! I think he's been eating out of dumpsters," Dad said. "We'll put him in the garage." After Dad led him to the garage, Mom found some old blankets and t-shirts and made a place for him to sleep. David and I spent the rest of the day going in and out of the garage checking on our new houseguest. All those presents I got under the tree didn't come close to what showed up on our sidewalk that morning. He was the best Christmas present ever!

The next day, Dad took the dog to the vet to get him checked out. The vet said he looked healthy and free from disease, so we took him home and gave him a bath. Dad said he could tell the dog had been eating trash because when he went to the bathroom Dad could see aluminum foil in his "you know what." When Mom told David and me that we could keep the dog, she asked, "So what's his name going to be?" My brother came up with some names, but I knew what I wanted. Boomer. Just like Boomer Esiason of the Bengals. He was the quarterback and everyone liked him. I wanted everyone to like Boomer the dog, too. Dad said Boomer had some bull terrier in him and also had some golden retriever and lab.

Dad thought Boomer probably grew up in a cage, because he acted like he had never seen stairs before. He was afraid of them. When he first came inside, Dad or Mom would have to carry him up or down the stairs. He also did not like to eat out of a dog dish, so I would sit next to Boomer's dish and feed him from my hand. At night, when I watched TV, I would use Boomer as my headrest.

Boomer and I loved each other. I told him that many times. Talking to Boomer all the time helped me learn how to speak better. Not only are dogs man's best friend, but they also are man's best teachers.

Even though we put flyers out for months trying to find Boomer's owners, no one responded to them. Sister Martha and I prayed really hard for Boomer to stay with me. One day though, almost a year later, a stranger knocked on our door. He had one of our old flyers in his hand. Dad answered and I heard the man say, "I lost a dog and I think you have him." I was afraid of losing Boomer and started crying. Dad told the man, "I don't think our dog is your dog. Besides, he didn't look like he had been taken care of very much." The man grumbled a bit and finally left. I told Dad that night how much I loved him for saving Boomer. Dad said, "Boomer's family! Besides, Boomer didn't even recognize that guy. He probably found one of our old flyers. There is no way anybody is going to take him away from us, especially someone who doesn't treat him nice."

Sister Martha always said Boomer was a gift from God. He helped me learn how to speak better and maybe even to love better. He lived until my senior year in high school. The year I graduated from high school was the same year Boomer died. He meant so much to me. He woke me up every morning, and waited for me by the front window until I came home from school. I think of him a lot and miss him so much. I love you, Boomer. Thanks for being my friend.

Chapter 6

I MADE MY BEST FRIENDS AT MERCY. EVERYONE THERE ACCEPTED me for who I was. I didn't feel different or out of place, even though for a while, I was the only one with Down syndrome in the school. Then when I was in my second year of preschool, another student with Down syndrome enrolled. His name was Chris Hemberger, and he was a year older than me. We weren't together in a class until fourth grade. Our teachers accepted us for our gifts and struggles and encouraged us to work at our own pace. Two or three grade levels are always combined in one classroom; that way we can learn from one another. That is the Montessori way.

Mom read me a book about Maria Montessori, the lady who started the first Montessori school over in Italy. Sister Aloyse also talked about Maria in history class when I was in 7th and 8th grades. Since I spent almost sixteen years of my life in a Montessori school, I know all about Maria. She was a beautiful lady who was a doctor and teacher in Rome, Italy. She tried to get a job as a regular doctor, but back in the late 1800s women were supposed to teach or get married. So Maria started a school for poor children who were behind in their education, or who had never been to school. She believed all children could learn, even those with special needs.

She taught practical life skills, like learning to wash dishes or grow a garden. She believed in using the sense of touch to teach language and math. Maria also believed children could create music from everyday utensils and tools, and she encouraged children to paint with their fingers.

I remember at Mercy Montessori we moved letters around in

a shallow box to make words. In math we used lots of colored beads. The beads were really numbers and each color represented a different one. For example, all the yellow beads were the number four, and we would put them together to make cubes and squares. That's how I learned addition, multiplication, and division. I even learned the square roots of numbers.

Patty Normile, the teacher I had after Sister Martha, taught me the most about math. She taught me how to count to 1,000 using strands of colored beads. At first, I had a hard time with the beads. They were divided into tens, hundreds, and thousands. When I finally got it, I knew how math felt. I had actually touched the numbers and held them in my hands.

Patty wanted me to answer in class like everyone else, but sometimes I would get lazy and try to sleep in class or gaze out the windows. Patty always reminded me to pay attention or stay focused. She would say, "Teddy, over here." That would make me smile, and I would get back to work. But sometimes I would have really bad days and refuse to do any lessons. Instead of getting mad, Patty would get out her Bengals cards and let me hold them. Then I'd be really happy and want to do the lesson. Or Patty would say, "If you don't do your work, I'll tell your mom, and you won't be able to watch *Baywatch*." That always did the trick for me! I really loved *Baywatch*. I still do! I used to hum the song all the time. When we go to the beach, I run into the ocean like the lifeguards on *Baywatch*. I'll ask Mom and Dad, "Did I look like Mitch?" Dad will say something like, "For a moment, I forgot it was you." My mother said I am the target audience for *Baywatch*. I think that was supposed to be funny.

Patty included me in everything she taught, even when I didn't always understand what she was teaching. I never felt left out because I had Down syndrome, and because of Patty, I made many friends. Besides Lauren and Renee, my closest friends were Teresa Riva, Christopher Ihle, Matthew Moore, and Lindsey Kellerman.

They always asked me to do things with them, and they even helped me with my schoolwork. They are still my good friends and we keep in touch. They sent me cards congratulating me for being the Good Will Ambassador for the Reds. Lindsey Kellerman is now a special education teacher at St. Bernard High School in Cincinnati. She tells everyone she became a special education teacher because of her friendship with me.

In first and second grade, I spent lots of time learning how to tell time and how to count money. Every morning for two years, Patty would place a penny, a nickel, a dime, and a quarter on my desk. She would ask me to name them all, and I could, except for the dime. Patty and the entire class clapped when I finally yelled, "Dime!" Instead of getting all excited, I just played it cool. "You've been asking me that for two years," I said. "It's a dime. I thought you all knew that. Helloooo!" I still have a hard time with money. Figuring out how much money I need to buy things can really frustrate me. It just doesn't make sense.

Patty also made us keep journals. Before I could write very well, Patty would write down what I wanted to say, and then using my pencil I would copy the words she wrote on the lines below. Then she would have me read what I wrote back to her. A lot of days I asked her to write "I love Boomer." Then she would draw a dog next to it for me. Patty would draw all kinds of animals for me. I had lots of dogs and horses in my journal.

One day when I showed up for school, Patty wasn't there. There was a strange man in our classroom. "Where is Patty?" I asked him.

"Well, she's out for a few days." He wrote his name on the board and told us, "I'm Mr. Mark." He was actually Mark Flashpohler.

I was really mad that Patty wasn't there and Mark was, and I started acting silly. When he gave us some work to do, I refused to do any. He walked over to my desk and asked me why I wasn't working. I said, "Patty and Sister Martha are my teachers. I only behave and do work for them."

"Well, okay, then," he said and continued to walk around the room. After class I think he told the office I wasn't working. He probably told them what I said, too. And they told my mom. When I got home, Mom was really mad at me. She said I was rude to my teacher. But no matter what she said, or how many Bengal cards he let me hold, or how much *Baywatch* I could watch, or how many times he made me sit in the green chair, I would not do any work for Mark. Patti came back a few days later, and my life was normal again.

It's funny how things happen sometime. Later on, in second grade, I joined the basketball team at Mercy. I went to my first practice and guess who was my coach! Mark Flashpohler. He was my basketball coach at Mercy all the way up through eighth grade. We became really good friends and still laugh about what a stubborn kid I once was. Now I know how wrong and rude I was. When I was 18, Mark invited me to play softball on Cincinnati's Unified Softball League. Now I say things like, "I only play second base for Mark," and it makes him smile.

Besides Patty, I had other teachers for special classes like gym and music. We had music every week and once a year we put on a play. In the third grade, our music teacher had us put on a play that takes place on a farm. Most of the songs were about corn and farm animals. My mom really liked that idea, because, since it was October, we could all wear the same costumes for Halloween. Most of the kids wore horse or chicken costumes, and we sat on bales of hay when it wasn't our turn to speak. I remember asking Mom, "What should I be?"

"Why not be something different?"

"How about a goat?" I liked goats ever since I saw one at the children's zoo.

My brother was listening and he said, "How about a pig? That would be funny."

I didn't want to be a pig. So, I thought about it some more. "A cow. I want to be a cow." Turns out I wore the only cow costume, and I had a big part in the finale. The whole class sang a verse that went something like "I guess I'll always be..." and I had to sing "Just a cow!" all by myself.

In every single rehearsal I concentrated really hard to hit the right notes, but with the music playing, no one could hear me. The class tried to encourage me to sing louder, and the music teacher tried to help by singing along with me. But I was still too quiet, and no one could hear me. Since I was the only cow, I would be singing by myself. During the final dress rehearsal, dressed as a cow, I was really scared. When it was time for me, to sing "Just a cow!" I froze on stage. No one could get me to sing.

Then it was the night of the play. The auditorium was packed with parents, and they were all filming with their video cameras. The lights were really bright, and my classmates were singing their hearts out while I stood silently in my cow costume. My heart was about to jump out of my chest as I waited for my big moment. Suddenly the piano got louder, and I walked to the middle of the stage. All the students began, "I'll guess I'll always be..." The music stopped, and I knew everyone's eyes were on me. This was my big moment. My parents and David were watching, and I couldn't let them down. I shouted, "JUST A COW!" as loud as I could. The crowd went wild and my classmates all ran up to me for a big hug. They didn't even bother to finish the song, because they were so excited for me.

And guess what; Mom did make me wear the cow costume for Halloween that year. She thought I looked so cute in it, but I didn't want to wear it. Back then, I thought everything had a place, and the cow costume was only for school. But you know how moms are. I was a cow for Halloween.

I don't go out for Halloween anymore, but I used to have fun dressing up. (Except when I was a cow!) Since I like sports, I would usually be a ballplayer of some kind. I have been a Reds player, a Cincinnati Bengal, and even a leprechaun from Notre Dame. I was a cowboy, a dragon, and yes, even a cow. Not like the ones on cartoons now. My cow costume had spots and a tail and big floppy ears.

On Halloween night, I would never walk very far from home. I have never been a fan of walking a lot. So Mom and Dad would go with me to a few houses in our neighborhood and then we'd go back home. Another reason I wouldn't go far was because of this one house down the street. I'll never forget the first time I went to that house. Dad suggested we go there. "Why don't we go to that spooky house on the corner?" I thought about it. I had heard screams coming from that direction. "He gives out lots of candy, I hear," Dad added. That helped me decide to go.

As we walked up the creepy driveway, I saw a man leaning against a tree. His arms had chains around them, and the chains were tied to the tree. His face was covered with brown animal fur. His hair was all messed up and he had on a torn shirt and pants. He didn't even have on shoes. And it was cold! I looked back at Dad, and he was smiling. To get to his house, I had to walk down the path that went to his front door. He stood a few steps off the path. I watched him carefully. He just stood there and kept his eyes on me. I thought he was going to talk to me and maybe say, "Trick or treat!" I was almost past him when he screamed like a crazy person. Then he howled like a wolf and started to run towards me. The chains tightened just before he could reach me. He stuck out his hands like he wanted to grab at my throat. He growled and pulled against the chains. I was so scared I screamed and threw my plastic pumpkin at him. All my candy was in there but I didn't care. I just wanted to run away and not get eaten. I made it out to the street where Mom and Dad were waiting. They had seen it all. I think Dad was smiling.

"Want to pick up your candy?" Dad asked.

"No way. He can have it."

We started walking back home. Mom said she would give me

some of the candy we had left over. Before we made it home, I heard a girl scream from the same yard. I hoped our werewolf neighbor didn't get her. The next day we drove by his house and there was candy all over his yard. And my pumpkin.

Chapter 7

SOMETIMES, EVEN NOW, I HAVE TO REPEAT MYSELF WHEN talking to someone who hasn't known me for very long. Learning how to say words has always been important to me. I was lucky Mercy Montessori had a speech teacher close to the campus. Her name is Pam Metcalf and we are now very good friends. She worked with me mostly on pronunciation. Every day during school, when I was in the lower grades, a teacher named Steve Hartman would walk me to Pam's speech class on the top of the hill. Sometimes he would even ride me up the hill in his car and buy a soda for me at MacDonald's. Pam's speech class was off the property behind St. Ursula High School, which was a long way for me. I've never been thrilled about taking long walks. When I was in junior high, my classrooms were up on the hill in what my teachers called the "Little Red Schoolhouse," which was closer to Pam's class. (The Little Red Schoolhouse isn't really little. It's a large brick house owned by the Mercy nuns.) I was thrilled because I wouldn't have to walk up the steep hill to speech class. Then Pam moved her office down to the school's main building, so instead of walking up a hill every day, I had to walk down one. Ugh. I guess she wanted me to get my exercise.

The "Flow Through Fund" helped pay for my speech therapy at Mercy. I also took private speech lessons twice a week after school. On those days, Mom and I would drive across town to another office. Those were long days, so we would always stop at Wendy's afterwards and get a chocolate Frosty. Mom never got her own

Frosty, so she would sneak a couple of bites of mine when I wasn't looking. I wasn't big on sharing then. Whenever she would ask me for a bite, I would say, "Just one spoonful, Mom. Just one." But she still kept asking for more!

Because I spent an extra year in preschool, I started 7th grade when I was 14. During the summer, they had arts and crafts in the Little Red Schoolhouse for us, and they even had a class there for computer skills. Mom signed me up for camp there every summer, even in junior high. It was an all day camp where we reviewed what we had learned in school that year, and we wrote essays on the computer. I always wrote about my trips to Hawaii with my grandma and grandpa. My favorite part of the day was after lunch. That's when we played baseball and soccer. Mark, Steve, and Mr. Kaiser coached our teams. My favorite sport was baseball, and Mark said I could hit a baseball a country mile. I wish!

I REALLY LOVED JUNIOR HIGH. ONE of the best things about it was sitting next to Chris Hemberger and working on projects together. We are still really good friends. About four years ago, Chris's preschool teacher, Yvonne Reissig, arranged for all of us to have lunch together. So twice a year, Yvonne, Chris and his mother, and my mom and I meet for lunch. Sometimes my former speech teacher Pam Metcalf goes with us. Our favorite place to go is the Cheesecake Factory.

Our school day was divided into three parts: Steve Hartman taught me language in the morning; I had history with Sister Aloyse right before lunch; and after lunch there was math and science with Mr. Kaiser. Then we had religion class taught by Sister Aloyse and sometimes Father Shappelle. I remember sitting there in religion class thinking about my last class of the day. It was either music or art, depending on the day. Sister Aloyse taught music, but Ms.

Hennig taught art. I loved art class, and it's because of Ms. Hennig that I took art in high school.

We had swimming one day a week, just like in preschool and elementary school. Most of us were on the swim team and Tom Grant, our swimming coach, let us practice and race each other. Swimming day was always fun, except for this one day in January when I was in seventh grade. It was one of the coldest days of the year, six degrees below zero. That's really cold, even for someone who lives in Cincinnati. Icicles hung from the trees and bushes, and there was a sheet of ice over the snow. We were all swimming around in the school's heated pool when the fire alarm went off.

"Everyone out of the pool!" Tom hollered at us. We stopped and looked at him. No one wanted to get out. Sometimes we would have false alarms. "C'mon! Let's go!" He started clapping and blowing his whistle. We realized this was real and we all climbed out of the pool.

"Can I go get my towel?" I had left my towel in the locker room.

"No! We gotta go!"

"I'm going to freeze!" I said to Tom.

"We don't have time, Teddy. I don't know if this is real or not."

So out we went into the freezing cold. Some of my friends had their towels. But I didn't! We stood there, jumping around and shaking and waiting for someone to tell us we could go back inside.

Tom was cold and wet, too. I heard him tell the teacher next to him, "I'm not sure which is worse, freezing to death or taking my chances with a fire." Finally, the "everything's clear" bell rang and we all ran inside. Every one of us jumped back into the pool, even Tom. After being outside in the freezing cold, it felt like we were jumping into a huge hot tub.

ONE OF MY FAVORITE TEACHERS IN junior high was Mr. Kaiser. I had him for both math and science in 7th and 8th grades. I always struggled with math, but in junior high I had an even harder time. While the rest of the class moved on, I had to sit at a table by myself and work with the math beads. Most of the kids in junior high didn't need to use the beads anymore, but I just couldn't get some of the math. Equations, geometry, and fractions were very frustrating. I got to the point where I could do some geometry formulas, like the perimeter of squares and triangles. And I could do the square root of some numbers. But equations? All those letters and exponents and subtracting and adding drove me crazy. I didn't care about finding X. Ugh.

One day I asked Mr. Kaiser, "Why are we trying to find something you already know?"

He smiled and told me, "Well, if you find it, it will help us when I don't know the answer."

"I guess so," I said. "But if I never find X, it's okay by me."

Most days I looked around the room and watched the other students writing things down and solving equations. It made me feel like I didn't belong. But then some days, we would take a break from equations and work on the computer. On computer days, I would get really excited. I loved working on the computer, because I felt like part of the class. Even though math was hard for me, I liked Mr. Kaiser. It would be a bummer to have math with a mean or boring teacher.

Mr. Kaiser's science class was a lot more fun. While Mr. Kaiser talked, we all took our notebooks out and wrote down what he said. Since I really couldn't keep up, he would make a copy of his notes for me. Sometimes for tests, he let me use my notes. That was really cool! The best days were when we would do science experiments with a partner. I loved lab day because it was always a surprise. One time, after we watched *October Sky*, we made rockets out of plastic Coke bottles and took them outside and set them off. When we launched ours, it went above the surrounding houses and even St. Ursula. I couldn't believe how high it went. Other times Mr. Kaiser would give us a mystery chemical, and we had to figure out what it was by doing a pH test or flame test. Mr. Kaiser always told us, "Like Homer's Mom said, 'Don't blow yourself up.'" We would look at him and wonder if he was serious.

When I was in the main building, Mr. Kaiser walked me uphill to the bus line every day after school. I really don't like walking much and certainly not uphill. Sometimes I refused to walk. He got me to move by threatening to pull my hair if I didn't walk with him. He said it jokingly, but I believed him. I hate having my hair pulled, even if it's just a little tug, so whenever he would hold his fingers out like he was about to pull my hair, I would behave and go with him to the bus.

Because of those walks every day, Mr. Kaiser and I became very close friends. That's why I was really excited to have Mr. Kaiser as a junior high teacher. In his classes, I would sometimes pretend I was a wrestler named Goldberg, a real World Wide Wrestling champ. In class, I would walk up to one of the other boys and practice a Goldberg move on them and wrestle the kid to the floor. Then I would pretend to pin him and shout, "I am the new WWW champion!" The rest of the class, and Mr. Kaiser, thought this was really hysterical, and we would all laugh about it.

I've kept in touch with Mr. Kaiser over the years, and—guess what—he is now one of the players on my adult softball team. When I play softball, I pretend I am Todd Frazier, though before I became the batboy for the Reds, I used to pretend I was Brandon Phillips. Sorry, Brandon!

Sister Aloyse was my other favorite teacher in junior high. I was in her class for three years. She really wanted all of us to be independent. She taught music and my favorite subject—history. When I first met Sister Aloyse, I thought she looked more like a grandmother than a teacher. She was much older than my other teachers, so maybe that's why she taught history. Before she came to our school, Sister Aloyse taught music at Mother of Mercy High

School. After coming to Mercy, she went to Bergamo, Italy, to learn more about Maria Montessori. She still teaches part time, even though she is '85 years young,' as she calls herself.

One day after school, Sister Aloyse told me she went to the same barber as my dad and me. I couldn't believe it! Actually, I didn't believe her at all. I thought she was just joking with me. So the next time I got my hair cut, I asked my barber, Carol Henggeler, about it. She said, "Yes, I know Sister Aloyse. I cut her hair once a month at the Mother of Mercy convent in College Hill. She talks about you all the time."

I was surprised, so I asked her, "What does she say about me?"

Carol laughed. "She says you're one of the nicest students she has. Some of her students walk in the room and don't say a word, but you always say, 'Good morning, Sister Aloyse,' in a bright, cheerful voice." She smiled and said, "You make her day, Teddy."

"She sat in this chair? And she said I make her day?" *Wow*, I thought. Then I turned to Carol. "What did you tell her about me?"

"Oh, just how I've been cutting your hair since you were five. And how I got you to sit still for your haircut. And how your mom tutored my daughter Molly with her reading."

"That's right! Mom tutored Molly!"

"Molly was nine then, and still had trouble reading. Your mom helped her a lot."

"I remember hiding from you when you dropped Molly off."

Carol laughed. "Do you remember the day I saw you peeking around the couch? I told your Mom, 'Now there's a big boy who needs a haircut.'"

I did remember that day. Mom told Carol that I hate it when people touch my hair. She didn't think I would sit still for a hair cut.

But Carol wouldn't take no for an answer. She told Mom, "He seems like a very well-behaved child. Let me at least try." Mom finally agreed, so Carol took me outside into our backyard. She knew I liked to look at the flowers and the trees outside, and thought that being outside might take my mind off the haircut. And it worked! She sat me in a little chair and gave me a handful of daisies from my mom's garden. Because I really liked holding the flowers, I sat very still for her and received my first real haircut. Carol always tells people she is a real barber, not one of those fancy hair stylists that work in a beauty salon.

Carol still cuts my hair. Sometimes she cuts it on Saturdays while I watch Big Time Wrestling reruns on TV. My dad usually watches with me because Carol cuts his hair, too. After our haircuts, my dad and I like to wrestle on the floor and pretend we are on the show. If Dad wins a point I shout, "You're the man!" Or I put Dad in a sleeper hold, and he'll fall down like he has passed out. Then I jump up and raise my hands. "The new World Champion is Teddy Kremer!" Mom always laughs at us. "Will you two ever grow up?" she sometimes asks.

"No way! I'm still a kid at heart."

One day Carol asked me who I thought the boss of the house was. Right away, I said, "My dad!" But Carol shook her head and smiled. "Your dad might think he's 'the man,' but your mother is the real boss of the house." She's right, my mom is the boss, of everybody. All of our haircuts go through Mom. Dad and I like our hair cut straight down, but Mom always wants it over to the side. So our hair has a part on the side. Carol has been cutting my hair for twenty-six years. Twenty-six years? That's a lot of hair.

Chapter 8

I REMEMBER SISTER ALOYSE'S CLASSES THE BEST BECAUSE SHE made learning so much fun. In history, we would begin class with our chairs in a circle and share current events and other important news. Then we'd move back to our tables and get our notebooks out. Sister Aloyse always had a presentation ready for us. We would listen, answer questions, take notes, and then do something really cool, like create a wall mural, perform a play, or make something out of paint and clay.

Sister Aloyse also taught us music in the seventh and eighth grades. In her class we formed a band made up of Orff instruments. The instruments were all different and very difficult to pronounce and spell. Sister Aloyse didn't care which instrument we chose, and she didn't make us play the same instrument all the time. I remember playing the xylophone, marimbas, glockenspiel, metallophone, and also the drum. (Mom helped me spell all the names except for the drum.) I had so much fun in that class. We would dance around the room as we played and then sing songs from the radio or our school song. We also practiced playing to hymns, because our band provided the background music for our school Masses.

It was during those band practices that I really started noticing differences between me and the other students, except for my friend Chris. Sometimes the boys would show off for the girls and act silly when they played the instruments. The girls, instead of telling the teacher, would laugh and start acting silly, too. I didn't get that at all. I didn't say anything to Sister Aloyse, but I know she wouldn't have liked all that silly behavior. And then, after all that, some of the boys would talk about girls in a way I didn't understand. One time in religion class Mr. Kaiser gave a talk about the sacred bond of marriage, and how sex is God's way of adding people to the world. He also told us that girls and boys should treat one another with respect, especially when we start dating. I've never really gone on a date, except for prom, and I've never had a real girlfriend. All my girl friends were just that—friends. I would like to have a girlfriend now, but so far I haven't found any girl I want to spend a lot of time around. I dance with girls when I have ballroom dancing, and some of them want me to be their boyfriend, but most of them are too old for me. I haven't given up. I'm still looking for "my girl."

I grew up a lot in junior high, especially in the eighth grade. My speech improved a lot and Mom said I became a whiz kid on the computer. It was a really good year for me in school. It was also the year Mom surprised us with an idea that turned out great.

EVERY DAY THAT YEAR AFTER HALLOWEEN I would come home from school and ask the same question. "Can we get our tree this weekend, so we can have the first one in the neighborhood?" Dad probably got tired of my pestering him about getting a Christmas tree, so the Saturday after Thanksgiving the whole family piled into our car to go tree hunting. We spent the night at my godparents' house in Sunman, Indiana, because Aunt Joan and Uncle Terry live so close to the White House Christmas tree farm.

We woke up early the next morning and it was snowing. That made it even better. I don't mind the cold as much as I do heat. So off we went with Aunt Joan and Uncle Terry to the middle of Indiana to the White House tree farm. It's nicknamed that because that's where President Lyndon Johnson bought his White House Christmas tree. The tree farm was so big that Mom and Dad brought along my Quad Racer.

I got the Quad for Christmas when I was seven. It's a small, electric car, and it made hunting for Christmas trees a lot more fun. I loved that car! I used it at home all the time. I could ride all over our neighborhood. One time, after I first got the car, I went all the way up to the house of a Cincinnati Reds player named Billy Dorn. Mom and Dad were looking all over for me, and they finally found my car parked outside his house. I just parked out front and knocked on the door. Mom and Dad rang the doorbell, and Billy invited them in. "Mom! Dad!" I said when I saw them. "I made a new friend!"

So while David and my parents walked all over the Christmas tree farm, I drove my Quad.

Because I was in my little car, I found a tree really fast. "How about this one?" I asked Mom. She always made the final decision about which tree to bring home.

Mom looked at the tree and shook her head. "Maybe, but we haven't looked long enough."

I knew what that meant. She was going to walk all over the farm looking for the perfect tree. Every year we would watch *A Charlie Brown Christmas* on TV, and Mom was afraid we would end up with a scraggly Charlie Brown tree. She walked forever looking for a tree. David and I were getting cold, so we asked Dad if we could sit in the car.

"I thought you guys wanted to help with the tree," he said.

"I do, but I don't think I need to see all the trees to pick one," David said.

Mom finally picked out a tree, and *boy* were we all relieved. Even Dad. We started walking to the car, but Mom said, "Hold on, I have an idea."

We all stopped and looked at her.

She told us with a smile, "We're going to get two trees this year. The extra one will be a cardinal tree, in honor of Colerain High School." David was a senior at Colerain then, and my dad was the assistant principal. Plus, I would be going there the next year, so it made sense to have a tree with the Colerain mascot on it. "Great idea, Mom," I said. "But my Quad's almost out of electricity."

"Leave it in the car. The exercise will be good for you."

Now we had to walk around looking for another tree. After about an hour, David and I went back to the car. I hate to walk; I'd rather swim.

Mom finally found another tree, and Dad tied them to the top of our International Scout. We didn't put the trees up right away, because Mom needed to find ornaments for the cardinal tree. That first year, she only found a few cardinal ornaments, but we have lots of them now. It takes forever to unwrap them and put them on, but once it's done, the tree looks really cool. It's full of red cardinals and little white Christmas lights. The best thing about having two trees is that they both have presents under them. My eighth grade year, Santa brought me a video game and new country music CDs. It was a great Christmas morning. I could play Madden football and listen to Keith Urban all day.

I love getting presents. Especially the ones Santa brings. I can hardly sleep the night before waiting for the morning to get here. I sometimes think I hear Santa, but I never get out of bed to spy on him. I'm afraid he might see me, and then I won't get as many presents. Every Christmas Eve, I always look out the window for his sleigh and reindeers. I still look for Santa and we still have two trees. We keep them up a long time. Christmas is such a good time of year. Everyone loves each other a little better, so why wouldn't we want it to last longer? I do. We used to get two real trees. Now one of our trees is artificial, because of my allergies. The fake tree looks great though, because it is covered in bright red cardinals.

ANOTHER COOL THING HAPPENED IN EIGHTH grade. Every year, Sister Aloyse has all her seventh and eighth graders participate in the National History Day project. Thousands of students from around the country take part in the event. Students are required to choose a topic related to that year's theme and then learn all they can about it. Students are allowed to use books in the library, surf the Internet, visit museums, interview people, and even look through archives. After picking a topic, students write a paper and then make an exhibit, build a diorama, or enact a scene from a famous person's life.

In seventh grade I chose to do a paper on Benjamin Franklin. I worked on the project with Chris Hemberger, the other student with Down syndrome in the class. Chris was a year ahead of me and graduated from Mercy that year, so in the eighth grade I worked on the National History Day project by myself. I don't remember much about my seventh grade exhibit, but I do remember almost everything about my eighth grade exhibit.

The theme my eighth grade year was "Turning Points in History." I chose Michael Jordan and the history of basketball. Other than Todd Frazier, Michael Jordan is one of the greatest athletes of all time, and the best basketball player ever! After I started reading about Michael Jordan and watching VCR tapes, I learned how important he was to basketball. He's an all-around cool dude. I really like his underwear commercials!

Here is some of what I learned. Jordan led the NBA in scoring for ten seasons and tied Wilt Chamberlain's record of seven consecutive scoring titles. I saw a picture of Wilt and he was really tall! Jordan also holds the top career regular season and playoff scoring averages of 30.1 and 33.4 points per game. His total of 5987 points in the playoffs is the highest in NBA history. He retired with 32,292 points in regular season play. The only players to score more are Kareem Abdul-Jabbar and Karl Malone. Jordan also played on two Olympic gold medal-winning American basketball teams. In 2009, he was voted into the Basketball Hall of Fame. He even tried to play Major League Baseball, but it didn't work out. But at least he tried.

After months of working on my paper, I decided to do pictures and stats of Jordan's career on a three-sided display board. I named my project "Michael Jordan, King of the Court." The show was at Miami University in Middletown. Several judges came to my display.

"So, Teddy, why did you pick Michael Jordan?" one of them asked me.

"I think he's the greatest!" I answered.

One judge looked at the numbers I had on the board. "Without looking at your display, tell me the years the Bulls won the championship."

I knew that! "1991! And they won the next two to make it a three-peat."

He asked me a lot more things, and I got them all correct. The judges smiled and shook my hand. "Well done, Teddy," a judge said as he walked to the next display. Lots of people came by, and I told them all about MJ. I did take a break to look at most of the other displays. I really learned a lot.

Later that day, the awards were announced. I waited anxiously for my name to be called, but I was not one of the winners, not even one of the runners-up. After the winners left the stage, the emcee announced, "And now, we want to give a special award to someone who did an excellent job on his project. This award goes to Teddy Kremer for his exhibit about Michael Jordan." He called me up in the front of the exhibit room and presented me with a check for 100 dollars. I couldn't believe it when the announcer handed me the check. I gave him a hug (of course). Then the audience applauded really loud. The announcer asked me if I wanted to say something. I did.

"Thank you for letting me participate in the competition. It was very exciting. I learned a lot from the other students." I looked out into the crowd. "I would like to thank all my teachers, especially Sister Aloyse, for never losing faith in me. It takes me longer sometimes, but I eventually get there. I will never stop trying or learning." I waved at my parents. "And I want to thank my mom and dad. They told me I could fly to the moon if I wanted. My dad says, 'Always aim for the moon, even if you miss you will land among the stars.' I'm doing my best to get there."

The crowd cheered as I walked back to my seat.

After I sat down, my mom asked me where I learned to speak in front of an audience like that. I said, "Mom, I learned that at Mercy Montessori!" I told her about the Toastmaster lady who came once a week in junior high. Her name was June Weekly, and she volunteered her time to teach us the rules of speaking in front of a group. Once we learned the rules, we would practice speaking in front of the class. We would always cheer for one another after we spoke. Between the cheering and the support from my teacher, it helped me feel okay in front of people. Now when I give speeches I am never afraid. I really like talking in front of people, especially large groups. I guess I like all kinds of talking. My friend Todd Frazier says he doesn't mind getting in front of people and talking, but many of my friends say they don't like giving talks in front of anybody. I don't understand that. Most people are friendly and want to hear what you have to say. Sometimes when I give talks to schools, I carry a little card that has notes on it. I do this so I don't forget what I really want to say. I learned that from June.

Our last project for Sister Aloyse had to do with our future. We had to write an essay and then design a poster board showing the kind of job we hoped to have when we grew up. Then we had to present our poster boards to the class, and tell why we chose that particular field to work in. I wrote that I wanted to be a singer on stage, because I loved music so much. My poster board had pictures of country western singers and characters from Disney musicals. My favorite movie of all was *Beauty and the Beast*, and I even sang some of the lyrics to my classmates.

I thought my presentation was really awesome and cool, but

Lindsey Kellerman received a standing ovation for hers. When it was her turn to present, she held her poster board backwards so no one could see it as she walked to the front of the room. Then she smiled at me and said, "I've decided to become a special education teacher because of my friendship with Teddy Kremer. We've been best friends since preschool, and we even rode the bus sometimes together. I can't imagine life without Teddy. I will miss him when we all graduate from Mercy. I might not see him every day, but I know we will always remain friends and keep in touch. Because of my friendship with Teddy, I hope to go into the field of special education.

"I want to make sure I'm surrounded with special people like Teddy for the rest of my life. Teddy is so full of confidence, joy, and kindness. Whenever I had a down day, Teddy would always give me a big hug. I want kids like Teddy to know that they are the world's greatest treasure. We at Mercy have been so lucky to have had Teddy in our lives all these years."

Then Lindsey showed the class her poster board, and she had a big picture of me pasted in the center of it. On one side she had written, "World's Greatest Treasures." The other side said, "Lindsey Kellerman, Special Education Teacher."

After Lindsey graduated from college, she took a job as a special education teacher at St. Bernard High School. And just last year, she had her students write essays and create poster boards showing what kinds of jobs they hoped to have. She modeled a board and essay for them, and guess who she wrote about! Me! But really, Lindsey is the special one. Her students are very lucky to have her as their teacher. For years, I've asked Mom what it means to be humbled. I would hear people use the expression all the time, but I didn't know what it meant. Mom tried to explain it to me, but I just couldn't get it. And then one day, I thought of Lindsey and how much she loved her students, and I finally got it.

Even though I had a loving family and great friends, I sometimes had lonely feelings. There were times when I would get so frustrated and wished so much that my brain would work like everybody else's. I did learn to read at an early age, and I know that I am lucky, because some of my friends with Down syndrome cannot read very much at all. Mom says for a child with Down syndrome to learn to read, he has to start early. Well, my mom started teaching me to read almost as soon as I was born, and then she placed me in Sister Martha's hands. And you know Sister Martha, once she makes up her mind about something, there's no going back. She was determined I would read. And I did.

Even though I spent years in physical therapy, I still can't write very well because of the weak muscle strength in my fingers. My teachers in junior high had to write things down for me, or let me Xerox their notes. I wish they had iPads when I was in school. It would have made life so much easier, especially in junior high.

Though I was excited to move on to high school, it was hard leaving Mercy Montessori. I remember Patty and Sister Aloyse standing together at the door on my last day of junior high. I wanted to tell them how much they meant to me, but I couldn't find the words. I started to cry. I knew I would miss them so much. They began crying, too. The next thing I knew, we were locked in a three-way hug. It was the biggest hug of all my years at Mercy.

Teddy's first birthday

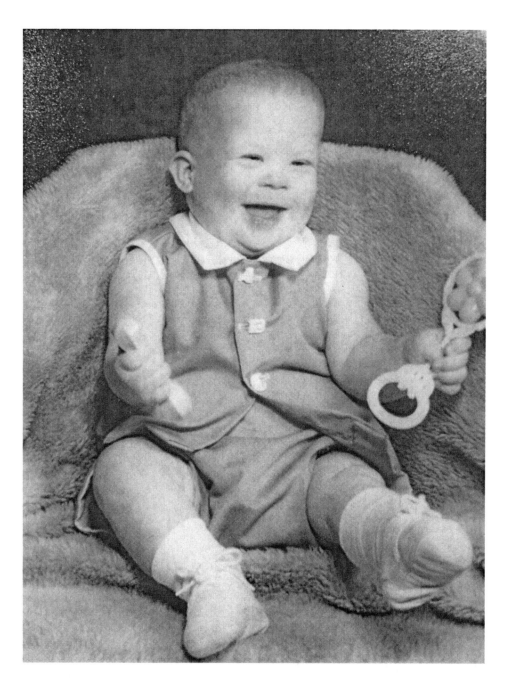

Teddy at three months

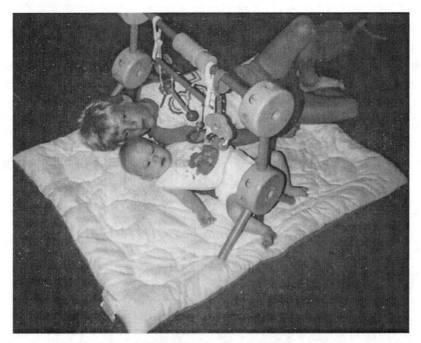

Teddy at four months and David at six years

Teddy's baptism at four months.
From left: Dave, Cheryl, Teddy, David, and Father Leo

Teddy at 14 months

Teddy at 21 months

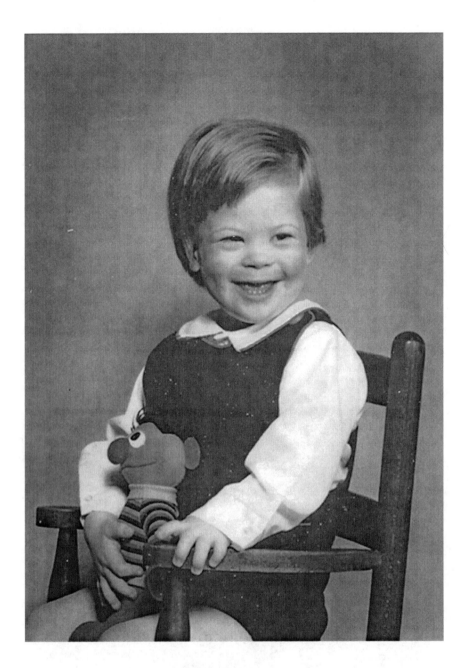

Teddy at two years

Teddy's first steps at two years old

David, Ricky, and Teddy (three years old) skiing

Teddy (three years old) and David

Soccer at age five

Sister Martha and Teddy (age five)

Teddy, David, and Mimi and Papa (age five)

Teddy (age six) and Cheryl

Teddy (age six) and Daddy

Teddy's First Communion (age eight)

Teddy's baseball photo (age nine)

Teddy (age 10) at Easter

Patty, Sister Jacinta, and Teddy (age 10), 1993

Teddy (Age 11) and Lindsey, 1994

Teddy (age 12) and Chris in Washington, D.C., 1995

Lindsey, Teddy, and Tiffany in Washington, D.C., 1995

Teddy (age 13), David, and the grandparents

Teddy (Age 14) with the Butler family, November 1998

Mercy basketball (age 14)

junior high (age 15)

Sister Jacinta and Teddy (age 16), graduation day 2000

Teddy, Family, and Mimi-Over-the-River

Chapter 9

SADLY, MY DAYS AT MERCY MONTESSORI WERE OVER AND NOW it was time for high school. My parents decided I should go to our district high school since Dad was assistant principal there. I had been to Colerain High School many times with my dad, but until I knew I was about to go there, I didn't notice how big it was. I wondered how I would make it to all my classes without getting lost! The size of the school really freaked me out. I knew I would miss Mercy an awful lot.

"What if I'm late to class?" I asked one night at dinner.

"We'll practice going to your classes," Dad told me.

That made me feel better. A little bit. I didn't really know too many people at the school. None of my Montessori friends went to Colerain. All my former classmates went to other high schools, including Summit Country Day and St. Ursula Academy.

At the end of July, Dad took me for a tour of the school and Coach Coombs was there. He's the head football coach, and he's been at Colerain a long time. He was in the front office when my dad and I walked into the building.

"Hey, Dave," he said to Dad. Then he shook my hand. "And how are you, Teddy?"

"I'm doing pretty good. But it's hot." I don't do well with hot. The news said it was one of the hottest summers in a long time. All I did was sweat. But it was cool that the head football coach remembered my name. I had talked with him before, and he was a super nice man. The football team was always really good, and I went to all the games when my brother played guard. By the time I started high school, my brother was already out of college, but Colerain still had the same coaches. That day Coach Coombs talked with my dad about the new school year, while I looked at the trophies in the hall.

Later, after Dad showed me around the school, we went to McDonald's for lunch. While we were there, Dad told me that Coach Coombs asked if I wanted to be part of the football team.

"Me? Why?"

"Well, he knows how much you like football. And you've been one of their biggest fans."

I nodded. I had yelled pretty loud when my brother played. And when we scored a touchdown, I would throw my arms up in the air and dance around.

My Dad looked at me as I ate my French fries. "He thought you might like to help with the coaching."

"Wow!" I was so excited. I couldn't wait to tell Mom. Then I thought about it. "What does that mean? Does he want me to be the water boy?"

"No, he said you could either be on the team or help with the coaching. Coaching doesn't mean being the water boy. Isn't that cool?"

"Cool?! That's crazy!"

"So, which do you want to do?"

Well, it was so hot that summer that all I could think about was the players running sprints and sweating. And, I wasn't sure how much playing time I would get. The coaches wore shorts and baseball hats. "I want to coach!"

"Your mom is going be surprised," Dad said.

"Coach Kremer!" I yelled. "How exciting is that? I can run through the banner and be on the sidelines and help Coach Coombs call plays."

Dad smiled, "Well, maybe the first two things."

Mom was thrilled when I told her. "What does that mean?" Sometimes Mom and I think the same.

I had no clue other than, "run through the banner and be on the sidelines."

Dad said we would go to school the next day and talk with Coach Coombs.

When we talked to Coach the next day, he said I had to be there when practice started in August. "You can help out and we'll see what works best for the team."

I enjoyed the rest of the summer, but I couldn't wait for practice. When practice finally started, it was really hot! At the beginning of every practice, Coach Coombs would have everyone together, and he would talk about why we had to work hard at practice. "If we want to win the state, we have to outwork everyone else!

At first I helped with water and equipment, but once I got to know the players and coaches, Coach Newton asked me to work with him. Coach Newton was the running backs' coach and I was to be his assistant. That means we were in charge of the fullback and tailback and how they run through the line and block for each other. Working with the quarterbacks wasn't one of our jobs; another coach worked with them.

For the first few weeks, I mostly watched and listened. Since Coach Newton was the head baseball coach and my brother played for him a couple of seasons, I already knew him. He also went out to dinner with my family a few times a year. I remember looking at the menu one time and asking the waitress, "How is this prepared?" Coach Newton thought that was funny.

We got to be even better friends during those football practices. He helped me when I didn't understand what he was teaching the players. The players told me some things, too. It took me a while to know what "hitting the edge" and "cut off your blocker's hip" meant. We practiced in the morning and then came back for another practice in the afternoon. Those kinds of practices are called "two-a-days," and they pretty much take up the whole day.

People with Down syndrome lose electrolytes faster than regular people. I learned that word—electrolytes—from my doctor. He made me write it down one day and I haven't forgotten it. So that means we need drinks with the right things in them for when we sweat a lot. And boy did I sweat at practice. I had to cut back on watching Disney during the day, but it sure was fun to be on the field with the players. Sometimes I would go home with Dad, but if he had meetings or activities, Mom would pick me up after practice.

A FEW WEEKS AFTER FOOTBALL PRACTICE started, school opened for classes. The day before school started, Dad drove me to school so we could pick up my schedule. He walked me to all my classes several times until he thought I could do it on my own. I left school that day feeling confident I wouldn't get lost the first day of school.

I knew that as soon as I arrived in the morning, I would go to homeroom for special needs students. All the students had homeroom before classes every day, and I was no exception. Then I would go to math class followed by history and English. After that I had lunch and then the rest of my classes. It was easy with Mom and Dad helping me. Plus, the halls weren't filled with students running all over. I knew my first day of school was going to be hard. My 8th grade class at Montessori had only fifteen students, but Colerain was a big high school. There were over 2,000 students in the high school. No more small classes for me!

My first day, Dad introduced me to the principal, Mrs. Schulte, and she was very nice. It made me feel even better when she said in her Southern accent, "Teddy, if you ever need anything, you come see me. Okay?"

"Yes, ma'am." With my dad already there, and the principal telling me she was there for me, and the coaches there to help, I felt I would be okay. I smiled at Mrs. Schulte and said, "If I can help you too, just ask."

She laughed at that and went on down the hall. "I'll probably be calling you soon, Teddy. Know any good math teachers I can hire?"

After that I went to homeroom and took a seat right in front of the teacher's desk. I opened my book bag and took out my notebook and pencils. I was as ready as I could be. All my teachers, Sister Martha, Patty, Sister Jacintha, and Mom and Dad did a lot for me in junior high and elementary school. Now I had to be a high school student.

The homeroom teacher wrote her name on the board, and told us that if we ever needed anything, or had any problems, to let her know. She also said we could stop by her classroom any time, since she taught in the same room all day. When she dismissed us, I went to class with regular students. Mom and Dad insisted I attend classes with typical students. My doctors told Mom that people with Down syndrome will act like the people they are around. In each of my classes, there were several special needs students and our inclusion teacher would take notes for those of us who couldn't keep up. Sometimes she would make up the tests we had to take. It made me feel good to be in a class with everyone else. I didn't want to sit in a room with a few other students while the rest of the school was out there together. Our school was on block schedule. We took four classes every day, each one an hour and a half long. If it got boring, it felt like three hours. I usually loved my classes. But not all.

I had one class without my inclusion teacher and it was really hard. It was a strength class where we would learn how to lift weights and use the exercise equipment. During that semester I was pressing more weight than the offensive line. Lifting weights was not my problem.

We also had to take notes on the parts of the body, especially the muscles and bones. I have a hard time using a pen or pencil, and the teacher talked so fast I couldn't keep up. Some of the girls in class took notes for me, but it didn't help. I remember the teacher asking me, "Teddy, why aren't you taking notes?"

I told him, "I'm a better listener than I am a writer." I didn't want him to know that I was in high school and such a slow writer. I told him I could remember things well, but he didn't seem to care. I finally told Dad about the class, and he had a meeting with my teacher as a parent, not as an administrator.

At the meeting, my teacher told Dad, "If he can't do the work then he shouldn't be in the class." Dad told him I was really trying. He also told him that I'm a really hard worker and that I have a very good memory. But the teacher still insisted that I take my own notes without any help. When dad told me what he said, I got so frustrated I wanted to cry. I secretly felt that my teacher didn't want to have a kid with Down syndrome in his class. I had experienced this kind of reaction before, but never from a teacher. It made me really sad.

I think dad felt the same way, because a few days later I was in another class. I'm pretty sure Dad had something to do with the change. I was glad to be in another class where the teacher was more understanding. He even seemed glad to have me. "I hear you are a smart dude," the teacher said that first day. He told me not to worry about taking notes, because he would make copies of his notes for me. After that, I felt better about things.

Funny that my weight lifting class would give me the most trouble. I thought it would be my math class. Actually, my math class was not the hard stuff like algebra and geometry. This class was a life skills math class. When my brother, David, heard about the class, he said he thought all high school students should take it. He said it sounded more useful than all those formulas and equations.

David was right. The class did help me a lot in everyday life. I learned how to tell whether I had a ten, five, or one dollar bill. I learned which bill was worth more. We also practiced our addition, subtraction, and division skills. When my grandma asked me what I learned in math, I said, "I learned about money." She laughed and slapped her knee. "Well, now you're ready for the real world, young man."

ONE DAY IN ENGLISH CLASS A student asked me, "Why are you in here?" He looked over to his friends and smiled.

"I'm Teddy. I went to Mercy Montessori for a long time. But I'm here now." I put out my hand. He just looked at me and went back to talking with his friends. Then Coach Coombs walked in to give something to our teacher. He saw me.

"Teddy! How's it going?"

"It's good, Coach."

He came over to my desk and said, "Don't be late to the coaches meeting this afternoon."

"Yes, sir." I looked over to the kid who had been rude. "I'm one of the football coaches."

Then Coach Coombs winked at me and left. I didn't have any trouble in that class again. Unfair as it is, we athletes do get treated pretty special.

I HAD MR. KALBLI FOR FOURTH block science class. His class was on the second floor. At the beginning of the year, I realized it was getting really hot in class. I raised my hand. "When do they turn on the air?"

Imagine my shock when he answered, "There's no AC here."

Auuugh! No AC? I hate being hot. As the class went on, it was all I could think about—just how hot it was. I couldn't pay attention. At least on the field I could wear shorts. But I always wanted to dress nice for school, so I had on long pants and socks and a short-sleeved shirt. My dad always made me tuck my shirt in before I went into the building. "You're the assistant principal's son, and you need to make a good impression." Sometimes I took my shirttail out, because I wanted to be cool. Then my dad would see me walking to class. "Teddy," he'd say, "Tuck your shirt in!" I would do it. By the end of my first day, my armpits were wet. Even my underwear was wet from all the sweat.

But Mr. Kalbli was really nice and I liked his class a lot. I think he volunteered to teach the classes with kids like me. The classroom was not set up as a science room. There was no special equipment for experiments, so Mr. K had to figure out how to do his labs without Bunsen burners, sinks, or test tubes. I remember we made a volcano out of baking soda. When it spewed out it was so cool.

Once I got used to sweating at school, things weren't so bad. I sat by myself at lunch, but after about a week I had made some friends. Every day at school I would eat the cafeteria food. I hear on TV people making fun of school food, but I loved it! People with Down syndrome usually have a tongue that's a little too big, so we like soft food the best. If food feels rough, I really don't like it. But the lunchroom ladies always knew what I liked, so they took care of me. They always gave me extra mashed potatoes and sometimes an extra cookie. They always had homemade chocolate chip cookies made by Miss Rita at Mom's school, Houston Elementary, where the school bakery was located. They delivered the cookies fresh every morning.

If I could get away with it, I would eat nothing but chocolate chip cookies for breakfast, lunch, and dinner. But when Dad gave me lunch money each morning, he told me to buy healthy food, not just cookies. He also told me that I didn't have to spend all my money. I could save some of it for an afternoon snack at Wendy's. But when I got in the lunch line and saw the hamburgers, I would try to sneak an extra one. If Dad was working in the cafeteria that day, he would take my second burger and eat it for his lunch. "Teddy, you don't need two hamburgers or two chicken sandwiches," he would say. "Or two sodas. And tuck your shirt in." But if he wasn't around, I would eat at least two hamburgers. But I know I really shouldn't have, because I had to see the cardiologist every six months, and I still do. People with Down syndrome have weight problems and cholesterol problems. Some people with Down syndrome have heart problems and I'm lucky I don't, but I do have a thickening of the muscle around my heart.

Even so, I always bought an extra cookie or Mom made me a peanut butter sandwich to eat after school. It helped me get through swim practice. By the time practice was half over, I'd be hungry again.

The cafeteria was a happy place for me, but not for everybody. In the years I was in school, some of special education teachers thought it would be a good thing for the special needs kids to clean up the cafeteria once lunch was over. I was supposed to help, but Mom and Dad wouldn't let me. When some of the kids in my homeroom asked why I didn't help clean up, something Mom said came back to me. So I told them, "I wouldn't mind if we took turns with some of the other kids. Why doesn't the Spanish Club or the football players help clean up?" I didn't mind helping, but I wanted to be more than just someone who cleans up after other people. I knew I could do more than that because my mom and dad, and teachers at Mercy, told me I could. And I believed them. It made me sad to see the other students with disabilities working in the cafeteria, picking up trash and scrubbing tables. Somehow, the teachers thought it was okay for special education students to work like custodians. I guess it's because they have had this cleaning program for years.

Mom said when she was at Colerain, the special needs kids worked in the cafeteria just like they do today. Why only special needs kids? Why not what some people call "typical" kids? Or even the gifted kids? My mom said everybody should take a walk in other people's shoes. And she also says schools should have high expectations for every student, not just some. I wonder how the custodians feel about only the special kids taking turns cleaning up. I bet they get their feelings hurt. And you know what? Our custodians are some of the smartest people in the school.

Chapter 10

WE HAD OUR FIRST HOME FOOTBALL GAME THE SECOND WEEK of school. I finally got to run out with the team through the banner. Coach Coombs went first, and then the rest of us rumbled past the cheerleaders. I looked up at my parents and waved. With the band playing and the crowd cheering and the players going crazy, it was more than I could take. I was jumping all around and banging players on the shoulder pads and high-fiving anyone I could. Even cooler, we won the game. My coaching record was 1-0.

That first season went by really fast. I watched and listened to Coach Newton a lot. By the end of the season I had learned how to make a handoff, how to block a rushing linebacker, and how to run a sweep. But the most exciting part was being on the field with all the players. We all became close friends, and I wanted to hang out with some of them after the game at LaRosa's pizza, but Mom wouldn't let me. I was even invited to a few parties, but that was a "no go," too. "Not this year," she would say. "But maybe when you're a junior or a senior." Even though I was sixteen my freshman year, Mom said I didn't have enough high school experience to go to upper grade parties. She knew most of the seniors and juniors because she taught them in elementary school, and she said they were all nice kids, but "teens will be teens." I didn't really mind missing the parties; the football games were way more exciting than any party could be.

That first year was so awesome for Colerain football. We even won the region! We got all the way to state playoffs, but lost against a team up north. I was sad when we lost our last game and I cried a little. But Dad reminded me that the season wasn't over yet for the Cincinnati Bengals. That cheered me up. I've been a fan forever.

My parents always bought season tickets to the Bengals games with my grandma and grandpa. They would take my brother and me to all of the games, even when we were really little. Our tickets were in the front row of the blue section of Riverfront Stadium, the best seats in the place. I remember getting to the games early and waving to the players as they came into the stadium. Some of the players would even come over and shake my hand. I got to see Boomer Esiason, and it made me cry when he went to play for the Jets. My parents told me about the "freezer bowl" back in 1982. I'm glad I missed that one. I mean really missed it! I wasn't even born yet. As you know, I don't like being too cold or too hot. We did go to some really cold games, though. I would drink hot chocolate and watch my breath steam out of me. I pretended I was a fire-breathing dragon. When it snowed during the games, it looked like fun to be out there playing in it. No one ever threw a snowball at the other team, though my brother, David, and I wanted to. It was so exciting when the Bengals won, but I would get so sad when they didn't. I sure did like it when we beat the Steelers, which we didn't do enough. I loved when we played Cleveland; the place would go crazy. I would jump all around and clap with my gloves on. Those were fun times! I went to Bengals games from the time I was five or six until I was a junior in high school.

ONCE FOOTBALL SEASON WAS OVER, I couldn't wait to try out for the swim team. Dad had taken me to meet the swim coach earlier in the year. The pool at the nearby sports complex where the swim team practiced was gigantic, especially compared to the pool at Mercy. But before I tried out for the swim team, something else happened that made for a great day.

One day at school, Coach Newton asked me what I was doing the rest of the year. I told him that I was going out for the swim team, and then in the spring and summer I played community baseball.

"Well, you know what, Teddy?" he said. "Why don't you help me with the baseball team this spring?"

Oh, wow! I thought. "I love baseball!" I told him. "That would be great." We shook hands and then I asked, "What would I do?"

I think Coach Newton and my dad had already talked about it. "I believe you need to be our bench coach."

"That is so cool," I said as I gave him a hug. Then I told him how I played Knothole baseball when I was growing up and how I could hit a baseball better than a soft ball. Usually, I played second base, but sometimes my coaches put me in the outfield. When I didn't have a game or practice, Dad and I would throw the ball at home. He would toss me pop-ups and grounders. But I had to take batting practice with the team. Mom didn't want me breaking a window. When I told Coach Newton about how I had played baseball before, he was even more excited about my being his bench coach. I asked him what my duties would be as a bench coach.

"When our team is at bat, the other coach and I will be coaching third and first base. So, you will be in the dugout making sure everyone knows when they're up to bat. And you can keep the guys fired up and focused on the game." He then told me about how I would get a jersey with Colerain on the front and how I could take balls out to the umpire. I stood very tall and said, "I'll do my best, Coach." I knew it was a big deal to be a bench coach for Colerain's baseball team.

I was so excited to know that I would be on the field with the team in the spring. As much as I loved helping with football, I knew I would love this job even more. I told Mom and Dad when I got home.

"Guess what!" I said.

Mom looked at me and said, "You've won the lottery."

I laughed at that. "No, but almost as good. I'm going to be bench coach for Coach Newton this spring!" I smiled all over again.

Dad patted me on the back. "That's great, Teddy." Dad knew how much I loved baseball. "That's going to make for a great end to the school year."

There was a long way to go before the end of the school year, but I didn't mind. I enjoyed every minute of the winter season, especially the snow and hot chocolate, and watching basketball and World Wide Wrestling.

Even though I struggle with some things, I can still do okay at sports. My strongest sport has always been swimming. I was on the swim team at Mercy Montessori and did really well in competitions. I competed in the Special Olympics at the state level and placed in the top three almost every time. My events were the freestyle and backstroke. When I swim, all I think about is getting to the other side. Nothing else but that. So I was excited the first day I met Coach Jenke. Dad took me to meet her one morning before school.

"Hey, Teddy," Coach Jenke said when she saw me.

"How does she know my name?" I asked Dad.

Dad winked at Coach Jenke. "I told her how much you like to swim."

"He said you were pretty good, too," Coach told me.

"I love swimming!"

"Well, are you going to come out for the swim team today?"

"Oh, yeah! I can't wait!"

I told Coach Jenke I wanted to do the freestyle and backstroke.

"That sounds good to me. I will see you at practice," she said.

AT PRACTICE, COACH JENKE BLEW A whistle to gain our attention. (It seems every coach has one.) Then we all gathered around her. I knew some of the other swimmers from my summer leagues and a few I had seen in the halls at school. Some of the upperclassmen looked like Tarzan of the jungle, and I couldn't help but sneak a peek at the girls. Coach told us how we each got a turn in our event. Then everyone jumped in and loosened up by swimming around for a while. My time to swim was later, so I had to get out and watch the others. The longer I waited the more nervous I got. Then Coach looked at me, "Teddy, you're up next."

I got in the pool and shook water out of my ears. Ever since I was little I have had tubes in my ears. People with Down syndrome are usually born with ear canals that slope the wrong way. So instead of water going out, it stays in. I used to get infections all the time until the doctors put tubes in them. Sometimes they would just fall out or if they were in there a long time, the skin would grow over them. I think I have gone through about a dozen pairs in my life.

My first practice race was freestyle. That's where you swim like you are in the ocean and a shark is chasing you. Coach had her timer in her hand and blew the whistle. I pushed off the wall and swam as hard as I could. I saw the swimmer beside me a little ahead and I tried to catch up. We made it to the other wall and turned around. I could feel my arms getting tired but I didn't let it stop me. The other swimmers were yelling at us and I even heard a couple kids holler, "C'mon, Teddy!" I stuck my hand out to the wall and lifted my head. A couple of swimmers were ahead of me but I beat several. I wasn't last! The guy next to me patted me on the back. "Nice swim!"

"Thanks!" I told him. "You were great!"

The rest of the week we did more races and workouts and I made friends with some of the swimmers. When Coach Jenke announced when our first meet was and that I was on the list to swim, I was so excited! When Mom and Dad picked me up from practice, I told them all about it.

"That's wonderful, Teddy!" Mom said. I know Dad was proud, too.

During the season I got to race in lots of events. I even swam relays. In the pool it didn't matter if I had Down syndrome or if I had a learning disability. It didn't matter if I had a hard home life or an easy one. It didn't matter if I was rich or poor. All that mattered was that I tried hard and swam really fast for the team. That season we cheered for one another and high-fived when we won. We all hugged one another when we didn't win. Mom and Dad attended all my swim meets. They cheered the team on whenever we won our relays or single heats. They were there when I won my first heat as a freshman. I remember waving and smiling at them. In my senior year, I won my heat against a really good swimmer from Hamilton High. He was one of our biggest rivals and I finished ahead of him. Now, that was something!

As much fun as it was to swim in high school, I still remember how people would act when I was little and Mom took me to the pool. I would see some of the other moms take their kids out of the pool when I got in. They might not say anything but they didn't have to. I knew what they were thinking. It was even like that in high school meets sometimes. I might take a little longer to get ready than the other kids and parents would say to the judge, "Why does he have to compete with our kids?" One time, the judge told a mom, "We could probably say the same thing about your kid, ma'am." I had to smile at that. Those kinds of mean words from adults made me try harder. Every time I raced, I did my best to show I belonged.

For practices the team and I rode a school bus to the Mercy Fairfield Healthplex. Even Coach Jenke rode with us. We had a great time. The bus driver played oldies music on the way there and back, and we all sang along. In December, he put on Christmas music. This was right up my alley, because I love to sing!

IN MY HIGH SCHOOL CLASSES I had to take tests just like everyone else, but my teachers often read the test questions to me. Sometimes

I would answer the question out loud, and they would write my answer on the paper for me. At first the highest grade the special education students could make was a C. My mom didn't think that was right, so she called the head of special education and had a conference with her. "If Teddy works hard and gets A's and B's, his grades should reflect that," she said to the director. Eventually, the school changed the rule, and those of us with special accommodations could make grades higher than C's. We had to work hard, of course, and score well on our tests. That's only fair.

Math class was really hard for me. When we got to word problems I thought I would go crazy. They just never made any sense to me. I heard other students saying the same thing, so I didn't feel too bad. When it comes to word problems, some people really struggle. Kids either love them or hate them. I had to take special math with Mr. Kalbli, so I could get away from word problems.

I remember one day in math class the girl sitting next to me looked sick. Her name was Beth. I asked her what was wrong. Beth said she felt bad because her dog died. Then I saw tears in her eyes. I knew she wanted to cry, but she kept taking notes. I didn't know what to say. I usually know what to do. I usually give someone a hug when they are sad. I think I give hugs for just about anything! People say I hug too hard, but how can you love someone too hard? I know my mom and dad love me. They are the reason I feel loved. I think there are lots of kids out there who don't feel loved and I don't want it to be someone I meet. So I hug them and tell them I love them. That's what I was thinking when I got up from my seat in math class and hugged Beth. My teacher didn't say anything, but I think he understood.

NOW THAT I WAS IN HIGH school, Mom and Dad dropped me off at home when I didn't have after school activities, which was almost never. One time when I was home by myself, I let Boomer out and then I went to check on him, and the door between the house and door closed and locked. So Boomer and I sat on the steps in the garage until Mom and Dad came home.

When Mom saw me on the steps, she said, "Why in the world are you outside without a coat?"

"I locked myself out," I said.

Mom looked at Dad and said, "Well, we're going to have to take care of this problem." And they did. Mom and Dad hid a key in the garage so it wouldn't happen to me again.

A couple of days after that incident, we got a call from the doctor's office. It was Dad.

I heard Mom ask, "How?"

Mom listened and hung up. "Dad said he'll tell us all about it when he gets home. All I know right now is that he needs stitches in his right hand."

Before dinner, Dad came in with a big white bandage on his hand.

I felt bad for him because I knew it had to hurt getting a needle poked into your hand. I hate needles. When I was little, sometimes I would get sick like all the other kids. But if I threw up a lot I would get really thirsty. Mom and Dad would try to get me to drink water but when I did, it made me sicker. Then they would have to take me to the hospital to get fluids. The doctor would stick an IV in my arm. But first, my parents and some of the nurses had to hold me down. I may have been sick but the sight of that needle gave me instant strength. I felt like the Incredible Hulk. Dad said it was like "trying to tie down a bear." I hate needles.

Anyway, Dad walked in with his hurt hand.

He sat down and asked Mom for a Tab. "Well, I had to get something out of my brief case before my meeting at the central office, so I threw my keys on the dashboard." He rolled his eyes. "The stupid keys fell down in the defroster vent."

Mom laughed. "So how did you cut your hand?"

"I heard them rattling around in there. They were down by the gas pedal."

I asked him, "You could see them? How?"

"Oh, it took me forever to find where they were. I tapped all around until I heard them jingling."

"Okay, so how did you cut your hand?" Mom asked.

"I pulled back the panel by the heater and I could see the edge of the key ring." He acted out the rest of it. "I reached in and grabbed the ring. I was so excited. But when I tried to pull my hand out it became stuck."

"Wow. Stuck?"

"Yeah, stuck. Then I panicked and I gave a big yank and my hand slid along the edge of the metal. There was blood all over. Some of the kids in the parking lot saw me; I thought one of girls was going to faint."

I know I would've fainted. I don't like the sight of blood, especially my own.

"I had to go back into the building and get someone to take me to the doctor."

Dad held out his arm and showed me his stitches.

I couldn't look; I hate anything that has to do with needles.

"Did you go to your meeting?" I asked.

Mom went to the stove and stirred some potatoes. "Forget the meeting, did you get the keys?"

"Yep." Dad turned to me. "And, no, I didn't make my meeting. I guess losing keys can be a real pain, huh? Want to see my stitches again?"

"No way!"

I didn't go with him when he got them out. I don't mind the doctor's office, but seeing stitches come out—no way.

EVERY DAY, WHEN I GOT HOME from school, Mom and Dad had chores for me to do. I had to take out the trash, sweep the kitchen, and unload the dishwasher. If we got a lot of snow in the winter, I would help David shovel snow off the driveway. That was fun because it always turned into a snowball fight. One time when my brother was home, I hit him in the back of the head and the snow went down his shirt. He started jumping around yelling, "It's cold! I'm gonna get you, Teddy!" I ran away laughing, and he chased after me. The more he ran, the further my snowball went down his shirt. He had to go inside and change shirts. Now I play in snow with my nephews; it sure does snow a lot in South Bend.

About once a week I had to clean my room. I am good about making my bed but not so good about my shoe closet. My room is always neat, but for some reason I can't keep my shoes organized. I really try. I will match my shoes all up and sit them neatly in my closet. But somehow they end up spread all over the place. I think there's a sneaky creature that comes in and throws my shoes everywhere. I used to blame my messy shoes on my brother, but once he left for college I had to find another reason. I still don't have one.

Even now, my shoes get all mixed up. One day this summer, Mom called down to me from upstairs. "Teddy, are you in your room?"

"Yes, why?" I called up to her.

"I can't find my sandals."

Within minutes, Mom was down the stairs and in my room. She opened the door to my closet. Piles of shoes covered my closet floor. It looked as if a bomb made of shoes had exploded in there. I didn't recognize half of them.

Mom reached in and pulled out a pair of sandals. "I have been looking for these for two days."

I looked at her with wide eyes. "How did they get in here?"

"That's what I would like to know. Teddy, you have got to do better."

I spent the next hour pulling out my shoes and matching them up and putting them back side-by-side. Most of them were mine, but I did find a pair of Dad's tennis shoes in there.

Not long after that, we were in a hurry to go to softball practice and I needed my shoes. I opened my closet and there was a mess of shoes on the floor. I tossed shoes everywhere until I found the right ones. When I finally got to the car Dad nodded, "I know. The shoe fairy got in there again."

I smiled at him. "And I'm not happy about it." Years later, as the Reds batboy, I had to keep the bats and helmets organized for each player. I guess I should be glad they're not shoes.

PRETTY SOON, MY FRESHMAN YEAR IN high school was almost over. I couldn't believe it. Football was fun and swimming was great but now it was spring and time for baseball. Coach Newton had told me earlier in the year that I was to be the bench coach. Not batboy but a coach! I also helped out at practice. He had me help him with infield practice and the equipment. I also ran back and forth to the baseball shed, gathering tools for cleaning up the field. I think Coach worked more on that baseball field than he did in his yard at home. Our field looked like a park. We had to pick up lots of rocks. I don't know where they come from, but the infield seemed to grow them. We were always picking up rocks. If a ball hit one, it could really mess up a play.

I had to keep all the bats in the right place and make sure all the foul balls got back on the field. But the real fun was during games. My mom and dad came to most of the games. Whenever we were at bat, Coach worked third base. I was the only coach in the dugout, so I had to make sure everyone knew when they were up to bat. Cheering the players on was also part of my job. That was the easy part. Sometimes I would take infield practice with the players, and even batting practice. Our best pitcher could throw really fast so I didn't bat against him. I knew if I got hit, it would hurt. We had a good team but we didn't win region or anything like that. Just being on the field in the spring was great though. And I didn't wander off like I did in lollipop soccer!

After baseball was over, it was time for summer. We took a trip to Disney World. I love Disney! I grew up watching Disney movies on TV so anytime I can go see Mickey, I feel very lucky. But like most summers, this one was over way too fast.

Chapter 11

THE WEEK BEFORE MY SOPHOMORE YEAR STARTED, DAD TOLD me he had asked the ladies in the attendance office if they needed any help. Mrs. Merkle, the head of attendance, said she would be glad to have me around. My dad made arrangements for me to work in the front office for second block. And boy did I love it! Part of my job was to sign in or sign out students checking in late or leaving early. I could get some of my homework done in there too, since it wasn't busy all the time. I was in regular classes for most of the day, so I always had homework. I worked in there the rest of high school, and had fun talking with people who came to the attendance window. By the time I graduated, I think I had met every person in the school.

Even though the same few students always checked out early, I never asked them why. I also had to deliver passes to students who needed to check out or come to the office for something else. All I did was knock on the teacher's door and walk in with the pass. Some students were glad to get the passes; others were not, especially those called to the principal's office. That first year I took passes all over the school. But our school has three floors, and I hate to walk up stairs. If I could, I would sneak on the elevator. One day I got a pass that was way down at the end of the third floor. Ugh! "Do I have to go?" I asked Mrs. Merkle.

"There's no one else, Teddy," she told me.

I took the pass and started down the hall. I was on the first set of stairs and one of the football players walked up past me. "Hey, John," I said.

"Hey, Teddy," he answered.

"Are you going to the third floor?"

"Yep. Why?"

"Can you take this to 312?"

He thought about it for a second and then said, "Sure. No problem."

Yes! I handed him the pass and took my time going back to the office. Mrs. Merkle was there.

"You did that quick," she said.

I just smiled and started on my health homework. The next time I had to go to third floor, I found someone going up there and got her to take the pass. This was great. I hated walking all over the school unless it was going down to the locker room. I thought I had it all figured out. Then one day I got back to the office after my plan worked again, and Mrs. Merkle looked at me with a grin on her face.

"What?" I asked.

"I know."

I tried to smile but all I could do was stare at her with my mouth half open. "Know what?"

"You keep pawning off the passes to the third floor."

So, I just told the truth. "I hate walking up there. It's too far. I'm sorry. It won't happen again."

Mrs. Merkle nodded and went back in the office. I don't think she told my dad. After that I only took "Teddy Passes." They were the ones going to the first and second floor. I guess my plan worked out after all. Back then I didn't want to walk up three floors, but for my job with the Reds I don't mind at all walking up the four floors to Fan Accommodations. I guess I've really grown up!

LIKE I SAID, I WAS THE manager for my high school football team. At the end of my freshman year, our quarterback told Coach

Coombs he wanted to play baseball only. He quit football and concentrated only on baseball, so he could make a college team and get a scholarship. I thought he should keep playing football because he was good, but he didn't come back. So, the backup quarterback was now the starting quarterback. His name was Sean. I knew who he was but we never talked much before he became the starter. We began talking during summer workouts. I was helping out at two-a-days and he was always there lifting. It was fun to hang out with him, but it was better when we became friends. Sean helped me so much. He treated me like he did all his other friends, and he made sure that no one ever picked on me. If he saw some of the players laughing behind my back, he would tell them to stop. "Teddy's cool," he would say. "He's one of us." The other players would claim they were just "dogging" me out, like they did everyone else, but neither Sean nor I really believed them. Sean told me that if you are really dogging someone out, you do it in front of the person, not behind his back. Because of Sean, most of the players started treating me with respect.

When I look back, I think maybe we helped each other. Once the season started, he sometimes would throw an interception at practice or in a game. He would run off the field and be mad at everything. He even threw his helmet a couple times and kicked at the water jug. I would go over to him and say, "It's okay. You'll do better next time." Sean might still be mad, but he would look at me and pick up his helmet. Then he might sit on the bench for a minute or hang out with Coach Combs. When he went back in, Sean would try his best to make up for his mistake. And he usually did. We had a great team and only lost one game each season he led the team. I was proud to be his friend. And the best part is, we are still friends.

Each week there would be team dinners at someone's house. Sean tried to make sure I was invited. He knew how much I loved those team dinners. But sometimes I didn't get asked. Coach

Coombs would get mad when he would hear about it. "Teddy's part of the team. He should be at every dinner!" But not all the parents wanted me there. I would hear the players talking about the dinners I missed, and feel really sad. Sometimes I would run out of the locker room, so no one would see me cry. Other times, I would pretend I didn't hear what they were talking about.

But most of the time, I loved being a part of the football team. In the locker room, I would get so excited about the game or practice. I would try to get the players just as excited as I was. They started calling me their favorite cheerleader. I really liked making them laugh, too. A couple of times, when the other coaches weren't around, a few players would get me to act really crazy. They told me to scream and run around the locker room. I thought it was okay, but then Sean would tell me to "bring it back in a little."

"They are laughing at you, Teddy," he said. "Don't do anything that doesn't feel right." That only happened to me a couple times. Most of the team was great to me. They loved how excited I became on game days. I even got to run around on the court with the team during pep rallies. Coach Coombs wanted me get everyone excited about the game. He's the best.

My sophomore year, I still helped with the running backs. If Coach Newton told them to hit the corner hard, I would remember that. "Hit the corner hard!" I would yell again and again. It was the least I could do to help the team. That's all that matters. The team. And winning. But the real coaches wanted us to be good people too, so I tried hard at that also.

Coach Newton always reminded the players that I was a coach and to listen to what I said. Sometimes a player would look at me and say, "You're not a coach. Why should I listen to you?" Coach Newton would hear this and give the player a firm look. He would say, "If Teddy asks you to do something, you better listen." He had a lot of confidence in me.

Game day was always so exciting. I would dress up for Spirit

Day, and during pep rallies I would jump around pumping my fists at the crowd. One of the parents had a "12th man" Colerain jersey made just for me, and that's what I wore not only for Spirit Day but also for all the games and pep rallies. I would eat with the coaches in the cafeteria but not say much. That was hard for me! Not the eating part but the not saying much part. After school we would meet in the auditorium, and Coach Combs would give a speech about playing hard and staying focused. If the players watched a movie, I would watch it with them.

Then it would be time for a meeting with Coach Newton and the running backs. I always gave them a pep talk. I would tell them the things Coach Newton told them. Things like "Stay on track in the option!" and "This is not smiling time!" and "Kick the edge!" He always told them to focus, and block and run hard. I would bang my fists on the table and remind them of what Coach Newton said. Then it was time to run out through the banner! It was so much fun. I miss those days of being with the players and hearing the crowd cheer. I was running back varsity coach for five years. Coach Teddy. Sometimes Coach Kremer.

During the games I would run up and down the sidelines yelling at the players. If we got a first down, I would point downfield like the referee. It was so exciting to be part of the action. I could hear the players huffing and hitting and running. When they ran hard into each other, it would sound like a car crash. I wondered how they didn't get hurt. But they would get up and do it again. Sean led us to be region champs and we were in the playoffs both years he was QB. When we would win, I would be so happy. In the locker room after the game, everyone would be high-fiving each other.

When we lost and were out of the playoffs, it was very sad to be in the locker room. I felt really bad for the players and the coaches, including myself. We had worked so hard all year, and now it was over. Just like that. It was a long, silent bus ride home.

During the years Sean was quarterback we had great teams.

But we didn't win state. When he played his last game, I was sad. Eventually, in 2004, the Colerain Cardinals won it all. Sean still lives in Cincinnati and works as a financial analyst for General Electric. Sean and I are still really close friends; we go out to lunch and bowling at least every few months. Actually, Sean was there two times I was batboy for the Reds, and he thought it was really cool when I hugged Todd Frazier.

AS THE YEAR CONTINUED, MY DUTIES in the front office grew. Sometimes I answered the phones, or helped a new kid find his classroom. During football season, I asked all the teachers who walked through the office if they were going to the game. "You better come," I would say. "We need as many people as we can get to cheer our team on!" I said the same thing to all the parents and students who stopped by the front office. It got to the point where almost everyone in the entire school knew who I was. One day the phone rang in the office. Mrs. Merkle answered it, and she then said, "Teddy, it's for you."

"Me? Who's calling me here?"

"He said he's from Elder High."

Elder High School was our biggest rival. They were usually pretty good, and it was so exciting when we beat them. We were playing them later that week. I took the phone. "Hello?"

"This is Coach Doug Ramsey."

Doug Ramsey! He was the head coach at Elder High!

"I understand you help out with the football team," he said.

"Yes, sir. I help coach the running backs with Coach Newton." I still couldn't figure out why he wanted to talk to me.

"Well, I just want you to know that we're much better than your team. And we will beat you as much as we can. No mercy. You tell your head coach that."

By the time he finished I was fired up. "There's no way you're gonna beat us! We are *so* much better and our quarterback is better and our fans are better!"

Mrs. Merkle watched me tell Coach Ramsey how we would be so far ahead at halftime his team would have no chance.

"Well, Teddy, you might say all that, but it's too bad for your team this Friday."

I couldn't stand it!

The guy added, "And if you don't start taking passes to the third floor, things will be worse."

What? How did he know that? Mrs. Merkle was smiling at me. Then I got it.

"Mr. Merkle! What are you doing?! You had me so mad." I started laughing because I was glad it was a joke. I handed the phone to his wife. She talked to him for a bit and then hung up.

"Sorry he got you so worked up, Teddy," she told me. "He knows how much you love our team."

I sure did. He got me on that one.

He called me more than a few times, and he got me every time. By the time I was a senior, it didn't take me long to figure out who it was on the phone.

Usually my school days were great, but not always. Like I said, my dad was an assistant principal at my school and his office was in the Career Center. Sometimes I would take the mail to dad's office. Most of the time, he didn't get much mail. One day though he had piles of mail. I scooped it all up in my arms, but some of it fell on the ground. Mrs. Merkle asked me if I needed help. Shaking my head, I grabbed the mail with my arms and walked into the hallway. Before I got past the trophy case, I dropped a few letters. When I tried to grab them, I dropped more. I got really upset and started panicking. I didn't know what to do, so I just sat on the floor next to the scattered letters. How would I carry all that mail without dropping it again? Then one of the football players came around the corner and saw me. He asked me what was wrong. Then he saw all the mail scattered around the floor. He helped me stand up, and we both picked up the letters and took them to my dad's office. Dad could see that I was upset, but when he started to ask me about it, I put my hand up. "I'm all right," I said. Then I turned and walked back to the attendance office. After that I took two trips if there was a big pile of mail to deliver.

Another day I was in the office drinking a Mountain Dew. Dad didn't want me drinking soda in school but I had one anyway. One of the other students working in the office saw me drinking my Mountain Dew. "Teddy, guess what we learned in science today; you shouldn't be drinking that."

I took my mouth off the can and asked, "What?"

"Drinking Mountain Dew can cause you to go blind. Completely!"

Mrs. Merkle shook her head, and said, "That's not true, Teddy. He's just joking with you."

I was glad because I really loved my Mountain Dew.

One of the great things about working in the office was that I could eat snacks and do my homework. Whenever I took a pass to someone near the cafeteria, I would snag one or two of Rita's cookies. They were so good! I would also stop by the pop machine and buy a Coke. One day I ran into Dad as I was heading back to the office. I quickly shoved the cookies in my pocket and held the can of Coke behind me. He didn't ask me about them so I didn't have to lie. I just can't lie to my mom or dad.

I helped Coach Newton with baseball again that spring. I always enjoyed being his bench coach, but the best part was hanging out with Coach. He has always been so nice to me and I know he didn't have to let me be part of the team, but he did. He is just a great guy! But finally, baseball season and school was over. I had all summer to watch TV, go to the pool, and play video games. And watch the Reds on TV. I knew every pitcher's record and every hitter's batting average. If I didn't get to watch the game, I would read about the game in the sports section of the *Cincinnati Enquirer.* Even when I was little, I learned all I could about the Reds. I remember cheering for them while sitting on the floor in front of the TV. They won the World Series in 1990 when I was seven. They had a great team in 1995 but lost to the Braves. By then I was really into the Reds. Every time they won, I cheered; every time they lost, I cried.

Chapter 12

MY HIGH SCHOOL DAYS HAD ALL KINDS OF SURPRISES. During the summer before my junior year, Dad told me I was taking home ec.

"Isn't that class for girls?" I asked him.

Mom didn't think like me this time. "Well, no it's not. Everyone should know how to cook. It's even better if you learn how to cook well." She looked at my dad and he nodded with a short grin. I remember when Mom was out of town and Dad had to cook for us. Maybe I did need to learn.

"I guess so," I told her. "But will there be any guys in there?"

Dad told me there would be for sure.

"Will we have to read cookbooks and make recipe cards for homework?" I asked.

Dad laughed. "I don't know about recipe cards, but it will be fun." Then he asked, "You know the best part about home economics class?"

I shook my head.

"You get to eat everything you cook, like cinnamon rolls." And, boy, are they good! The students always bring some to the office whenever they make them.

That was all I needed to hear. Cinnamon rolls taste so awesome. I could eat them and chocolate chip cookies for breakfast, lunch, and dinner, if Mom would let me.

My fears about home ec went away after the first week. It turned out to be a great class. We would do book work for a day, and then have demo day. Then we'd actually get to cook! On cooking day,

I was in a group of four. Each of us had duties. At first I had to wash dishes, but then the teacher let me mix things and put them in the oven. I would watch through the oven window and ask about a million times, "Do you think the cake is done?" We also made pancakes, and yeast bread, and pretzels just like they have at the Reds game. But the day we got to make cinnamon rolls was a great day. Just like Dad said, they smelled so wonderful. You have probably figured out that I like to eat. I loved all the things we made in home ec. Well, maybe not the veggies. As good as the cinnamon rolls were, I liked the chocolate chip cookies the best. There's nothing as good as a chocolate chip cookie right out of the oven.

Sometimes in class I would get frustrated, though. I remember when my group said I had to wash dishes. I told them it wasn't my turn. "Teddy, Susan is out today, so it's your turn again."

"No way!" I said. Then I sat down at my desk and pretended to read my home ec book. Mrs. Lewis came over and asked me what was up. "I am not washing dishes," I said to her.

"Well, then you get a zero for the day, Teddy."

I didn't move. I remember folding my arms and looking away from my teacher. "I am not washing dishes!"

She tried again to get me to help the group. "Teddy, your team needs you to help."

The more she talked the more I made up my mind. I shook my head and then told her, "I'm telling my dad!"

She said, "Okay, have it your way, Teddy."

By the time I got home from football practice, I had forgotten all about home ec. Mom picked me up that day, and after a snack, I went downstairs to the family room and watched television. At dinner that night, I knew something was up, and that something was not good. After Mom passed me the mashed potatoes, she said, "Mrs. Lewis told your dad about what happened today." I looked at my mashed potatoes and gulped. It turned out my threat to tell Dad was not the best idea.

Before I could get "I wasn't..." out of my mouth, Mom jumped in.

"You were very rude to your teacher, Teddy. And to your teammates in class."

"But..."

"And you will help out next time by washing dishes. We don't want you to be treated differently by anyone," she said as she looked at Dad. "Do we?"

Dad said, "No we don't, Teddy. And so that means you cannot tell someone that I'm going to bail you out of trouble. If people treat you poorly, I want to know. But if your teacher expects you to do your share, then you have to do just that."

Mom and Dad waited on me to speak, but I just sat there staring at my plate. Then I started to cry.

"Don't you want everyone to treat you fairly?" Dad asked. "Teddy, you know that's the very thing we have been fighting for your whole life."

Then I felt really bad about how I had acted. In class the next day, I gave Mrs. Lewis a hug and told her I was sorry. I told my group I was sorry, too. I learned a good lesson in home ec.

MY FAVORITE CLASS MY JUNIOR YEAR was art. Mrs. Getz, my art teacher, was really nice and taught us how to draw and make things out of clay. She told us about a really exciting project that all students do in Art I. She said we were going to paint a picture of ourselves. She called it a self-portrait. I wondered how my self-portrait would turn out. I told Mrs. Getz I didn't know if I could paint a self-portrait, but Mrs. Getz told me not to worry because she would help me every step of the way. "Besides, Teddy," she said. "You need to learn all about art first. It will be a while before we get into self-portraits." Over the next few weeks she taught us art concepts, like perspective, design, and vanishing point. Many times I became confused and tried to listen more carefully. When she told us about seeing railroad tracks that look like they meet in the distance, I started to understand perspective and vanishing point.

Some of the kids in class didn't pay attention all the time. I thought they were rude to the teacher, but I didn't say anything to them. When Mrs. Getz told us about famous painters, I thought some of their paintings were really cool. We looked at magazines with artists in them. I really liked Salvador Dali because he painted melting clocks. And Leonardo Da Vinci was an inventor and a painter! He made the first flying machine. But when we had to do a report on an artist, I chose Edgar Degas. Do you know why? He painted horses!

I've always loved horses, and one of my favorite television shows is *Walker, Texas Ranger*. In 2005, I started horseback riding, and still compete in the Special Olympics equestrian events. I compete in both Ohio and Kentucky. So you can see why I was so excited to tell the class about Degas. Horses are so cool!

Before we did our self-portrait, we were asked to bring in something from home that we could draw. I brought in a small Cincinnati Bengal's helmet that Dad bought for me at one of the games. Mrs. Getz had us look at our object from several views. She wanted us to see the shadows and shiny spots. I saw things I never knew were there. She showed me that what I thought was white was probably many different shades of lighter colors and what I thought was black was really dark blue. I tried to draw the little helmet, but it was a lot harder than I ever thought it would be. Every time I would try to make a curve or straight line, it never turned out right. I got frustrated and I am sure I made a couple of funny faces about it. Mrs. Getz said I needed help with my skills. That's when she would have me trace rolls of tape. It helped me practice working with a pencil and being careful drawing curves. In the end, my helmet looked like a loaf of bread with a strap across the front. I did get the stripes right.

Finally, Mrs. Getz said we were ready to do our self-portraits. We studied this artist named Chuck Close. His paintings of himself are really, really big. And they are so cool. Each face was made of little squares that didn't look like Chuck at all. But when you step back and look at them, there was Chuck! I thought they were amazing and got excited about painting my face. I asked Mom how I should look. Should I wear a Reds hat, comb my hair back, have a smile on my face or have a serious look? Mom said, "Just be yourself." And, that's what I did. I wore my shirt tucked in and combed my hair to the side, business as usual.

As we were getting close to doing our self-portraits, Mrs. Getz took our photos, and then she did something on the computer so our faces were made of little squares. Each square was a different color. All I had to do was paint over the colored square with a matching color. I couldn't wait to start. And I really wanted to show my mom and dad. The hardest part was finding the color to match the square. I worked on it for a class period, and the picture looked all wrong, like I was sick or something. Then I painted over some of the squares, and ended up looking like I had sunburn. Making the right color was hard! Someone at my table said, "Your portrait looks like a Klingon!" The entire class laughed, even me. Then I finally got the colors right, and my own face started to show up. It took me several days of class to finally finish it. My teacher was thrilled and I couldn't stop smiling. I kept looking at my self-portrait. "I did that," I told people. Mrs. Getz let me take it to my other classes, and my teachers were almost as excited as I was.

"You didn't do this," one teacher said. "This is wonderful! And it looks just like you."

"It is me," I told her.

"I know that. But it's just so good." I gave her a hug for saying that.

The rest of the semester we got to do lots of art. I never thought this class would be so great, but it was. I couldn't wait to go to class each day. But sometimes class wasn't fun. The other kids in class were not as excited about art as I was, and they made the teacher upset about once a week. I remember one time when Mrs. Getz yelled at the whole class. She usually was so nice and now she was telling us we had done something wrong. I didn't know what I had done. I always tried to do what she asked to do, even though I knew my art wasn't the best in the class. The more she fussed at us, the more upset it made me. My eyes started to water and then I was crying in class. I had to run out into the hall. She followed me out and asked why I was crying.

"You're mad at me," I told her. "And I don't know why."

She closed her eyes for a moment and then smiled at me. Then she shook her head. "I'm not mad at you, Teddy. How could I be? You're the best behaved student in the class."

I sniffed and wiped my eyes with my fingers. "But, you were yelling at all of us."

"I'm not really mad at them. I'm upset with their behavior. They're good kids." She touched my arm. "But I am most certainly not mad at you. Okay?"

I nodded.

She gave me a quick hug. "Tell you what, Teddy. Next time I fuss at the class, you ask me if I'm yelling at you."

"I can do that."

We went back into class and everything was fine.

A few weeks later, we got yelled at again for not doing our work. I waited until she was done and then I raised my hand.

"Yes, Teddy?"

"Am I doing okay?" I waited for her to answer. I think she was thinking back to what she told me.

She smiled and said, "Yes, you're doing fine."

I ran up and gave her a big hug and went back to working on my next painting.

"You sure hug hard, Teddy," she told me. I smiled big.

One day Ms. Getz told me that a painting I did won an award and would be in the Hamilton PTA Reflections magazine. Usually the winners get to have their art go into the state contest, but not mine. Since I was a special needs student, the people running the state said I couldn't be in with the other students. They told my teacher, "Those kids have their own category." I was fine but I think Ms. Getz was upset. I know she tried to get the art folks to change their minds. My mom said, "I thought things were different now." That was in 2002, which is a long time ago, so maybe now they are different. You might think liking someone's art is all that matters. But I guess not for some people. For me, art class was so much fun, and I hoped I would get to take Art II the next year.

ON FRIDAYS IN THE LUNCHROOM THE students near me talked about who was coming over to their house that weekend. Other times they would mention parties at their house. Or talk about going to a movie on the weekend. I love going to movies. They would say to each other, "We're having this great party around my pool this Saturday. I can't wait!" I might hear, "Let's all meet at Regal tomorrow night. The new *Lord of the Rings* is out." Even though I heard them, I pretended not to because I knew they weren't speaking to me. I just kept eating my lunch. I knew they weren't going to ask me to go. It didn't bother me much, but it would've been nice to have a classmate say, "Teddy, how about it? Want to go with us for pizza?" I would've been excited to go.

I really enjoyed my days at school talking with my teachers and learning new things and then going to practice. But after that I went home and watched TV or read the sports section of the *Cincinnati Enquirer*. I remember thinking that my classmates were all out having fun at the movies or eating pizza while I was at home. Maybe they thought I would say something wrong or not know how to pay my bill. And they might have been right. Luckily, I stayed pretty busy with swimming and dancing and horseback riding. I also played a lot of video games. I spent many weekends visiting my brother, David, in Indianapolis with Mom and Dad. Boomer was always there for me too, so being at home was just fine.

The only friends who ever invited me to spend the night were Lauren and Renee Roedersheimer, my friends from Mercy Montessori. They have always been so nice to me. We had lots of fun at their house watching TV, eating pizza, and playing with their dog, especially on New Year's Eve. Then my whole family would spend the night, and David would even invite a friend. They were the only people who were not family that asked me to spend the night. Even after Lauren and Renee moved away, they still asked me to spend the night. Sometimes that even invited my family and me to their lake house in Tennessee.

I stayed a lot with my Aunt Sue and Uncle Greg. Mom says I started spending the night there when I was about three years old. I don't remember that, but I do remember all the fun things we would do. When I was eight, my aunt and uncle started taking me on camping trips in Brown County. One time as we were passing through Nashville, Indiana, my Uncle Greg stopped to get some kerosene for our camping stove. Next to the supply store was a country western shop and right in the window was a black cowboy hat. Uncle Greg saw me staring at it and said, "Teddy, that hat was made or you." So he bought it for me. It was just like the one Walker, Texas Ranger wore.

At the campground, there were woods and a walkway and a hill where we could see for miles. I loved going there, especially when we would sit around the fire at night and roast marshmallows. My aunt and uncle would tell stories, and I would tell them about school and all my sports. In the mornings we would go hiking on the trails, but I don't like to walk very far. So Aunt Sue and Uncle Greg bought me a three-wheel bike that fit in the back of their car. Then I could ride all around the park and talk to all the other campers. I even got to know the rangers. My uncle told me one time, "You've never met a stranger, Teddy." I told him I just like to talk to people.

As much fun as it was being around the camp and throwing the ball with Uncle Greg, at night it could get creepy. We would sit by the fire and I could hear things walking around in the bushes near us. Aunt Sue tells me all I would do is ask, "What was that?" over and over. Despite all the monsters near us, it never kept me from going back the next time.

Aunt Sue and Uncle Greg had a pool at their house. You know I love swimming! I was so excited to go over there in the summer. I could swim back and forth all day long or until it was time to eat. We would cook hotdogs in the backyard, and they tasted so good after I had been swimming all day. I think the coolest thing I did in the pool was lay on the bottom. I can hold my breath for a really long time, maybe a couple of minutes. At first I would practice in the shallow end so I could stand up if I got scared. Once I got okay with it, I would move to the deeper water and lie on my back looking up at the world. Aunt Sue was shocked I never needed a mask. "How can you open your eyes underwater? It bothers me," she would say. I don't know how I could do it, I just did. I would lie there for as long as I could, come up for air, and do it again. It was so interesting to see how different the world looked from the bottom of a pool. I figured that's how fish see us when we are standing on the dock at Brown County Park trying to catch them. No wonder I can't catch one! One thing I had to be careful about was being in the sun too much. I hate getting sunburned. I don't ever tan; I just turn red.

If we didn't have hotdogs at Aunt Sue and Uncle Greg's, we would go over to a nearby Mexican restaurant where I could get the Grande Platter. It was great! The plate had a little bit of everything on it. Uncle Greg always said, "Teddy, there's no way you can eat all that." But I proved him wrong every time. I got the same thing so much the people there knew what I wanted. "Hola, Teddy. You want the Grande?" I would smile big and give them a loud "Yes!" When I find something I like to eat, I order it over and over, like breakfast burritos and nachos and salsa. Sometimes Sue would let me help her cook lunch. My favorite was making tacos. At home Mom cooks most of the time and I don't help much. When she's gone, Dad and I might put something in the microwave, but that's about it. I know if I really wanted to make something more complicated I could, thanks to home ec.

Sometimes my parents and I go to dinner together at Aunt Sue's and Uncle Greg's. There is a basketball goal nailed to a pole on their street. Uncle Greg, Dad, and I would go out there and shoot baskets. A few guys in the neighborhood would come over and shoot with us. They always let me play in the games, because I was good at shooting and rebounding. We also played lots of cards at their house. I love UNO even though it would drive me crazy when I would be down to one card and forget to say, "Uno." Uncle Greg would say, "You didn't say Uno," and I would have to take a card. Arrrgh! Sometimes I would have one card left, and Sue would play the "Take 4" card. But it sure was fun when I did it to them. If I had to draw a bunch of cards, I had a hard time holding all of them. When I got too many, I sometimes would drop them. That made me upset so Uncle Greg built me a little wooden tray with slits in it where I could put my cards. My nephews Trey and Cord use them now. When Uncle Greg won, he would throw down his last card and lift up his arms and say, "Another amazing win by the all-time champion of UNO!" That meant we would play again because I couldn't stand losing.

I have always enjoyed going to visit my aunt and uncle. Staying overnight with them really helped me learn how to be on my own. We even started a Christmas shopping tradition. Every year they take me Christmas shopping so I can get presents. At first, we would just shop for my brother and Mom and Dad, now I shop for my nephews and sister-in-law, too. My aunt always asks me if I have a list, and I always shake my head, "No!"

"Teddy, how will you know what to get everyone?"

I tap my head and say, "It's all in here." When I want to get clothes for someone, I usually know what size to get them. Uncle Greg sometimes calls Mom and says, "Teddy says David wears an XXL. Is that right?"

Mom always tells him, "That's right. Teddy knows, so just go with it."

Uncle Greg is the one who pays for the clothes, but with my money! I have been working ever since I got out of high school, so Mom and Dad give Uncle Greg my money to spend. If I had to figure out the money at the store, it would take forever. Afterwards, we go back to their house and my aunt and I wrap the gifts. This is always as much fun as buying the presents, but the most fun is handing them out on Christmas!

Even though none of my classmates ever came over to visit, lots of my brother's friends did. David spent a lot of time with Richard, one of the guys on Colerain's football and wresting team. He would drop by after practice and eat dinner with us. Before we ate, Richard and I would get down on the floor and wrestle. Right there in the living room. Mom would say, "Don't break anything!" So we'd move Dad's chair and the table up against the wall. We had carpet and it would sting like crazy if he grabbed my legs and pulled me.

"You're going down, Teddy!" Richard would yell.

"I'm not Teddy, I'm the Kremernator!" Then I would jump on his back and he'd spin around. He was a champion wrestler, but I could pin him. He probably let me win but no matter, it made us hungry. Richard is now the Athletic Director at Lakota East High School in Cincinnati.

"Okay, Live Cincinnati Wrestling is over for tonight," Dad would tell us. My brother and Dad would laugh the whole time Richard and I wrestled and rolled on the floor. It sure was fun. Even when David came home from Butler, he would invite his friends over to our house, and we always ended up in a wrestling match. I guess that's why my mom always put up her Waterford before they got there. My brother and I don't wrestle much anymore, but my nephews love to wrestle.

ONE DAY DURING THE SPRING OF my junior year of high school, my dad asked me at dinner if I wanted to play softball. Dad said Mark Flashpohler, my teacher from Mercy, called and asked if I wanted to play on the Unified Softball Team. My dad explained the team was part of the Special Olympics, and some of the adults on the team had Down syndrome or other disabilities. The other half of the team was made up of people without disabilities or "typicals."

I said "Yes!" before I took another bite. I was excited that not only was Mark the coach, but he also played on the team. Dad told me that Mr. Kaiser and his oldest son Eric were on the team also.

The league plays games every Tuesday at a field not that far from my house. You have to be at least 18 and know how to play softball. There are nine teams in the league, and they are sponsored by businesses in the community.

At the end of May, Dad and I drove over to the field so we could meet the players on my team. The infield was all dirt and there was a backstop with benches on either side of home plate, but no place for spectators to sit. The outfield needed to be cut badly. It sure didn't look like the Great American Ballpark, but no one seemed to care. Everyone was just glad they got to play ball.

"Hey, Teddy," Mark said when we walked up. "Glad to hear you want to play."

"This will be fun," I said. I looked around and saw guys there whom I had known for a long time. We knew each other from other

Special Olympic sports. I liked the guys and girls a lot, and even though some were older than me, we were good friends.

"Hey Teddy," my friend Tommy called out to me. Tommy was shorter than me and didn't have much hair. One thing he did have was a smile. I shook hands with Tommy, while coach and my dad talked.

"Hey, man, how's it going?" Tommy asked. "I think Coach is going to let me catch today."

"Good for you," I said. "I don't like to catch. I'd rather play second or third. I bet you're good at catching."

Tommy nodded his head and gave me a big smile. "I try hard." He leaned close to me and tilted his head. He smiled again. "Are you going to play on our team?"

"I think so."

"Our team has been playing together for years. You'll really like the guys."

I heard a jingling noise and turned to see a guy whom I later found out was named Chris. He had a bunch of keys stuck to his belt, so when he walked, he jingled. "You playing?" he asked. "We could use another third baseman."

"I'm not sure, Chris. I have to ask the coach if there is a spot for me."

"Teddy!" my dad yelled. "Come here a minute."

I walked over and Mark put his hand on my shoulder.

"Welcome to the team, Teddy."

"When's our first game, Coach?"

He looked at his watch. "In about fifteen minutes."

"What?! Dad, I need my glove!" He gave me the car keys and I ran off to the parking lot to get my glove out of the car.

When I got back, Mark gave me a yellow shirt to wear. It had a Big Boy on the front with "Frisch's" written underneath it. Lucky for me, I wore my Cincinnati Reds hat to the game.

Mark said, "Teddy, you're at second base. Go out there and I'll throw you some ground balls."

I hustled out to second just like Pete Rose used to do. At least that's what my dad told me about Pete. He was known as Charlie Hustle. My dad gets all upset because MLB won't let Pete in the Baseball Hall of Fame. I feel sorry for Pete.

Coach Mark rolled some grounders to me, and I threw them to our first baseman.

After we warmed up, the umpire yelled out, "Let's play ball!" I was very excited to be in my first softball game in the Unified League. My side was up first and I was batting seventh. Alex was our leadoff batter, and he didn't do too well. He said, "The pitcher's coming in on me! He's trying to hit me." But the umpire didn't think so and called, "Strike three!" The other team got us out pretty quick, so I didn't get to bat until the next inning.

After we finally got the other team out, Mr. Kaiser was first up to bat and he made it to first base. Then it was my turn to bat. I took a big swing at the first pitch and hit it to third. The third baseman threw it to second, but Mr. Kaiser was there before the ball hit the second baseman's glove. I didn't see any of this because I was running as fast as I could to get to first. And guess what; I got on base! In my first at bat! I bet Pete Rose didn't get a hit his first time up. Maybe he did. I'll Google it later.

Chris, my friend with the keys on his belt, was up next. He hit the ball and got on base when the shortstop threw it over first. You could hear him running, but then he got tagged out going to second. Mark said, "If you weren't so weighed down with all those keys, you would've made it!" He was kidding with Chris and we laughed. Chris just smiled and went back to his spot on the bench.

The game was close and I had to field several balls. I threw one guy out and almost turned a double play. The game went by fast and we won 7-4. When the game was over, we shook hands with the other team. Everyone said "good game" to one another. Coach Mark asked Dad if he wanted to play, and Dad started playing on the team. He played for about three years, until he had rotator cuff surgery. It wasn't even a baseball injury. Dad fell walking David's dog, Esiason, in the snow. Dad is now the scorekeeper for our team.

When we were leaving, Tommy patted me on the back. "Good game, Teddy. I'm glad you're on our team."

"Me, too, Tommy."

"This sure is better than sitting at home by myself," he added. "I wish we could play every day."

Dad asked Tommy if he needed a ride home.

"My sister's coming to pick me up. I'll wait over here for her." He walked to the road and stood there looking for his sister. When we left I rolled down my window and yelled, "See you next Tuesday, Tommy!"

He waved at us and smiled his big smile. I forgot to tell you that Tommy was over 60 years old. That's old for a person with Down syndrome. He enjoyed every day he was alive. Tommy died a few months ago. People say that those of us with Down syndrome smile a lot. Tommy sure smiled a lot. I miss him and his smile very much.

I sure had fun that softball season, even when we lost games. Our record wasn't too bad: eight wins and nine losses. I still play in the league and Dad still keeps score at all the games. He is our biggest fan.

We're not in the Big Leagues, but I bet we have as much fun as the Reds, or almost as much fun.

Chapter 13

FOOTBALL WAS FUN THE FIRST THREE SEASONS, BUT DURING MY senior year, football season was over-the-top crazy fun. Even before the year started, we knew we had a good team, and sure enough the season started with a win.

Homecoming week was really exciting, because our team was undefeated. Each day leading up to homecoming, the spirit committee planned something special to get us excited for the big night. One day we all wore our favorite college shirts. I put on my Notre Dame sweatshirt and some people loved it and some not so much. Another day was camouflage day. Kids borrowed their relative's military clothes, and some kids wore hunting outfits. I don't hunt and I don't think I ever will, but it was fun to wear my brother's old camo pants and his orange sock hat. My brother didn't hunt either, but when he was in high school, camouflage clothes were cool to wear.

During the week, every class and club decorated shopping carts. Yes, shopping carts. I think most schools have floats for homecoming week with people riding on them and throwing candy out to the kids. But at Colerain we decorated shopping carts from the nearby Kroger store. Some groups might spend a couple weeks putting red and white banners and streamers all over their carts. And then during the parade, they would push them down the street. It was a long way, too. I never pushed any of the carts but Dad and I would watch. During halftime of the homecoming game our principal would announce who won the cart contest. Every time I would go with Mom to the Kroger, I wondered if we were using one of the carts from homecoming.

After homecoming, our football team continued to win. The stands were full at every game, and even my grandparents and my aunt and uncle came to the games. They were so exciting to watch! Sometimes David and his friends would come home from college just to watch Colerain football. We were as tough as any college team, and more fun to watch, in my opinion. We went undefeated in the regular season, but lost in the state playoffs. Go Cardinals!

Life seemed dull for a while after football season. It was really a letdown after all the excitement. Thank goodness for swim team and music class. Music class was one of my favorite classes; it actually was a choir class. It was really cool, because my teachers Michael and Randi Parks were married. I've known them since I was little, because my dad used to work with them. When I showed up for class, Mr. Parks said that I was going to be part of the choir. "Maybe one day you can try out for a role in a play."

I said something like, "Well, I don't sing in front of people much any more."

He and Mrs. Parks just smiled and said, "Who knows what you'll do?"

You got that right, I thought, thinking back to my days at Mercy, and my singing debut as a cow.

My dad had told Mr. Parks that I was to get no special treatment. I had to learn the songs and sing my part just like all the students. That was only fair. But as it turned out, I really liked singing in the choir and learning all the songs. I think that's when I developed my love for musicals. To this day, there are some songs that I just can't stop singing, like "Beauty and the Beast" and "Defying Gravity," but you know that already.

The great thing about Mr. Parks is that I could tell him anything. He knew that I liked a girl in the class named Alison. She ran cross country, and I would tell him that she was my girlfriend. He would ask me, "Does she know she's your girlfriend, Teddy?" I would smile big and nod, "I think she does." He would smile and say, "Close enough, I guess." So with Alison in there, I really couldn't wait to get to choir practice.

I always felt safe in that class and everyone accepted me for who I was. That didn't happen all the time. I remember a few times when I would be having a bad or sad day before I went to choir, I would walk in and not want to talk to anyone. Instead of going to my seat, I would head to the back of the room and face the wall. At first my teachers would ask if I was okay, and I would just shrug my shoulders. I don't remember what happened on those days, but I would be very upset and frustrated. Mr. Parks remembered that I liked Alison, so he would ask her to help me. She would take me back to my seat, and everything would seem better. Mr. Parks asked me one time if I stood in the back to get Alison to talk to me. I kind of shrugged and tilted my head. "I'll never tell," I said.

The year in choir went on with its fun days and singing. One day Mr. Parks announced to the class that there would be a musical put on by his classes in the spring. He said we should all try out for a part. I was really pumped. I was not shy about getting up in front of people, especially after being in the musicals at Mercy.

"What's the play?" someone asked.

Mr. Parks pulled out a comb and started to brush back his hair. "Guess which one."

I had no clue. We all just watched him comb his hair. Then someone yelled out, "*Hairspray!*"

Mr. Parks shook his head. He combed his hair some more. "*Grease!*" He stopped and put his comb in his pocket. Mr. Parks held out his arms wide and sang, "You're the one that I want, oooh, oooh, oooh, Baby." Everyone cracked up. Well, as it got closer to tryouts, I asked Mom if she thought I should try for a part. It was during breakfast and I was eating my favorite breakfast burrito.

Mom said, "Well, Teddy, why not? After all, you played Elvis in one of the plays at Mercy."

"Oh yeah, I remember that. I taught myself how to snap my fingers that year."

"Yes, I remember the blisters you had on your fingers. You stayed up all night practicing."

The next day at school I told Mr. and Mrs. Parks that I wanted to try out for the musical. They were thrilled. But Mr. Parks said, "We can't just give you a part, you have to earn it. Tryouts are this coming Monday."

Boy, was I nervous. I had to sing for a part in front of everyone. My classmates were always supportive. We always cheered for each other. I had sung in front of them before, but nothing as major as this. It was like I was trying out for the QB job and had to beat out Sean. There was a part in the play where I could sing "All Shook Up" the way Elvis did it. I thought it would be so cool to be Elvis. You can't get any better than that. After all, I was born on Elvis's birthday, January 8.

When the day came, I combed my hair back and pretended I was Elvis. Using my Elvis moves, I sang the words to "I'm All Shook Up." It wasn't the whole song but most of it. I was tired from all that dancing around. After I finished, everyone clapped and cheered. A few days later, Mr. Parks announced to the class, "And our Elvis is Teddy Kremer." My friends cheered again. I was so excited!

Now that I had the part, I had to practice. And practice. One day Dad said to me, "I sure love what you're doing, Teddy, but I will be just fine if I don't hear 'All Shook Up' again for the next decade." Dad was always trying to be funny like that. Ignoring him, I kept practicing and before long, it was the day of the play. The week before, Mom had found a fifties black leather jacket for me, and some grease for my hair. When we went to school the night of the play, I had on black shoes, a white shirt, and jeans. I slicked back my hair, put on my Elvis outfit and was ready to go. The play started and when it came to my part, I played my guitar and wiggled my hips like Elvis used to. The crowd went crazy. At the end of the song, I took a small bow and then joined the rest of the cast on the stage.

After the show Mr. and Mrs. Parks gave me a hug. They were as excited as anyone there. Mr. Parks shook my hand and said, "You know, Teddy, I was thrilled to have you in my class this year. But more than that, we've never had a special needs person in one of our shows. You're the first. And you did a solo!" I thanked him and Mrs. Parks for letting me be part of the play. "Oh, we didn't let you," he told me. "You earned it just like any other kid would have to."

A few years ago, Mr. and Mrs. Parks asked me to come back and be part of a fundraiser at Colerain. Since the mascot is the Cardinals, the fundraiser was called Dancing with the Cards. My ballroom dancing instructor came with me and we danced the waltz for everyone. I had such a great time. Before we left, I gave Mr. and Mrs. Parks a poster with my picture on it. I wrote on the poster, "Thanks for being part of my life." I really meant it.

That spring, I helped Coach Newton coach baseball again. But this year, Coach asked me to throw out the first pitch on opening day. Lots of my friends were coming to see me, so I asked Dad to practice with me in the back yard. When the day came, I was very nervous but I tried not to let it show. I walked out to the mound wearing my pullover shirt with Colerain on it. I wound up just like a Reds pitcher and threw a strike! The crowd cheered!

Standing on that field in the warm sun made me feel like I was in the Major Leagues. But not every day turned out so well. There was one day that still makes both my mom and dad groan when it comes up. It was during practice and Coach Newton was hitting infield practice. The equipment salesman came to the field and yelled, "I've got those shirts you ordered. It's too heavy to bring down." Since I was near the backstop, I jumped up and said, "I'll help him, Coach." The baseball field was really far from the parking lot. I knew it would be a long way to carry boxes.

Coach had this really cool vehicle he called the Gator. I had seen him use his Gator lots of times, and I thought it would be easy to drive. So when the salesman asked me to drive the Gator to his car, I thought it would be okay. The Gator was like a golf cart—or, I thought, like my little four-wheeler—but it had a place on the back to carry equipment. So we went to the baseball field to get the Gator. The salesman said, "You can drive us." I guess he thought I had driven it before. So I started it up and drove along the narrow path to the parking lot. Everything was going along great. We made it to the lot and the guy pointed to his car. As I drove towards his car, I suddenly realized I didn't know how to put on the brakes, or if there were any. Then the salesman started yelling at me to stop. Coach told my mom later that he could hear someone yelling, "Stop! Stop! Stop!" about the time he heard me slam the Gator into the side of the car. The baseball players heard the crash too, and they all ran to the lot and jumped the fence. By the time they got there, it was too late. I had dented the salesman's minivan.

When Mom came to pick me up that day, Coach Newton told her about the Gator incident. "We had a slight problem, Cheryl. Teddy ran the Gator into a minivan and tore up the back fender. It wasn't his fault though. The sales guy asked him to drive it, and Teddy thought he was doing the right thing."

Mom offered to pay for it, but Coach Newton said it wasn't my fault, and the uniform company insisted on taking care of it. Phew! I really dodged a bullet on that one.

THERE WAS ONE THING THAT HAPPENED that made my life in high school complete. All year long, the kids in my class talked about our senior prom. As a senior, I really wanted to ask someone to go with me but I didn't know how. I asked Mom and Dad about it.

Mom said, "I don't think that's a good idea, Teddy." Something made me think she was afraid no one would say yes, and I would get my feelings hurt. But I have never let someone saying no stop me, so I kept bugging her about it.

"Your dad is going to chaperone. Why don't you go with him?" she asked me.

I was on the prom court and really wanted to go. But not with my dad!

"That will be so lame," I told her. "This is such a bummer."

I thought more about it but couldn't get up the nerve to ask anyone. And I sure didn't want to go with Dad. Then Mom had a change of heart. One day I saw her on the phone talking with someone. Mom was talking to her friend Sue Roedersheimer. They were talking about what moms talk about, stuff like cooking, favorite restaurants, traveling, and of course their kids. She told Sue how I wanted to go to prom, but she thought I should go with Dad. I overheard Mom tell her how I didn't have a date for the prom. I overheard Mom say, "Okay, call me back."

In a little while, Sue called back. Then I heard Mom say, "Really? Do you think she would? Great, I'll have him call her."

Mom put the phone down and said, "Teddy, I have an idea. Why don't you ask Renee to go to prom with you?"

"What if she says no?" I asked. Now I sounded like Mom. "She goes to a different school."

"I know, but she knows lots of people at Colerain."

"That doesn't matter. She still might say no."

"Well, you won't know till you ask her. Besides, you bothered me for a week about this. And now you're chicken?"

That did it. Mom can't call me chicken. But I was nervous about it all of a sudden. What would I say when I called? I had no idea.

At dinner I asked Mom and Dad to help me practice asking Renee out.

Mom said she would help. The next day she wrote down everything I should say to Renee. I practiced and practiced. Finally,

I picked up the phone and called the Roedersheimers. I was so nervous, I felt like I was back on the bottom of the pool holding my breath.

Sue answered the phone, and I asked to speak to Renee.

"Of course, Teddy," Renee's mom said.

Before I had a chance to wonder how she knew it was me, Renee was on the phone.

"Hi, Teddy!" Renee said. "How is your senior year going?" She caught me off guard, because her question was not part of the script Mom wrote for me. So, instead of answering her, I read, "Renee, this is Teddy. Would you go to Colerain's prom with me at Paul Brown Stadium? It's May 22nd, and my dad and I can pick you up."

She didn't say anything for a second. Then she said, "That would be great, Teddy. But I can drive."

I looked at Mom and yelled, "She said yes!"

Wow! I was going to prom with Renee. She is smart and pretty, and really funny. I was so excited I don't even know what I said after that. We hadn't practiced what I would say next. So I just hung up the phone.

THE NIGHT OF THE PROM I was nervous and excited. I wore a black tuxedo with a silver cummerbund and silver tie. Mom said I looked like a movie star, and I couldn't stop looking at myself in the mirror. I thought I looked pretty good too, like I was all grown up. I was ready an hour before we had to leave, and I think I drove my parents crazy. I kept checking to make sure my bow tie was straight, and that my hair looked okay.

Finally, it was time to go. Since I don't drive, Mom and Dad drove me to Renee's house in Dad's Buick. When we got to Renee's house, I walked to the door by myself and rang the doorbell.

Renee's Mom let me in and I waited for her in the living room.

When Renee came down the stairs, I couldn't believe how beautiful she looked.

"You look like a princess," I told her. And she really did. I couldn't believe I was going to prom with her. I gave her a corsage and put it on her wrist.

"Thank you, Teddy," she told me. "You look pretty handsome yourself."

I smiled really big. Her dad said, "Why don't we go outside for pictures."

Mom and Dad were standing outside waiting for us. Dad had his camera ready, and we posed for pictures.

Then all of us, including Renee's parents, went to dinner at Prima Vista. That's a nice restaurant that overlooks downtown Cincinnati. After dinner, the Roedersheimers and Mom went to the Reds game. Renee and I followed my dad to Paul Brown Stadium in her gold Mercedes. When we walked in, everyone stared at us. I was so proud to be with the prettiest girl at the prom. We sat with my football buddies, and they teased me all night about my "hot date." Renee didn't seem to mind and even said she thought my friends were cool.

While I was sitting with Renee, one of the cheerleaders walked up to me. "Teddy, can I have the next dance?" she asked.

I looked at Renee and she said, "Go ahead."

So I danced with that girl, and then another senior girl asked me to dance. Then another girl came up to me, and then another. They kept asking me, but I started saying no, because I wanted to spend more time with Renee. And who wouldn't?

Later on, I was part of the prom court, but I didn't become king. I was okay with that because for the first time in my life I had a real date.

After prom, we went to a party sponsored by the PTA at an indoor sports complex. They had an ice skating rink, along with a basketball court and a climbing wall. I didn't get home until after

4:30 in the morning. Between the dancing and then skating I could barely move my legs the next day. But wow, did I have fun. And I owe it all to Renee for saying yes.

A few years later, Renee took me to a frat party at Wake Forest University. She was a cheerleader there and I got to hang out with all the college kids. Some of them were crazy but we had fun. We stayed up most of the night, and I even had an O'Doul's, after all I was twenty-two. I sure did sleep a lot after that trip.

For years, the Roedersheimers and the Kremers would go to Norris Lake for a summer trip. Dad would rent a boat and we would go tubing and hang out on the lake.

When I would be lying on the tube, Dad would say, "Alright, I'm about to go faster!"

"I'm ready!" But I never was. It always felt like my arms were about to come off.

Renee got married a few years ago, and I was not only part of the wedding party, but also I was given the honor of walking Sue, Renee's mother, down the aisle. The wedding took place on Daniel's Island, near Charleston, and I got to ride on an airplane again. All the groomsmen wore different colored socks, and Chris, Renee's fiancé, gave me Bengals socks to wear. He also gave us all pink ties to wear with our gray suits. If I thought she looked great at the prom, she was even more beautiful at the wedding.

I went to the groomsmen's party the day before the wedding and I had the most fun with Chris and his friends. One thing we did was play beer pong. That's where you try to throw a ping-pong ball into a cup and if you miss, you have to drink a beer. I told Chris I couldn't drink and he gave me a cup of water. But some of the guys were drinking and they got real funny when they tried to throw the ball. I got in the game and it was harder than it looked. I couldn't get that stupid ball into the cup no matter how much I tried.

"Ok, Teddy, if you lose, it costs you something," Chris told me.

"Okay, okay. Give me one more chance," I said.

"Since you're not drinking, you have to take off your shirt if you lose the next game." Chris thought that was fair and I was okay with it.

I gritted my teeth and gave the cup a good look. I tossed the ping-pong ball and it hit the rim and bounced away.

"Augh!" I said and got ready for my next toss. That one also hit the lip. I shook my head and moaned. "You need to miss!" I told Chris when he was about to throw.

He made it on the first shot.

I took off my shirt and everyone cheered. But I wasn't finished. "I want to keep trying," I said.

"Okay, sure," Chris told me. He looked to his friends. "What next if Teddy loses?"

One guy yelled, "Pants!"

I said, "No way!"

"Head dunk!" someone else said.

I looked at Chris. He smiled and told me, "If you lose you have to dunk your head in the ice chest full of cold water."

I thought about it and then stuck my hand in the water. It was cold! Well, I hate to lose, so I nodded at Chris and said, "If I win, you have to do it."

We shook on it and the battle began. He missed and then I missed. Then I went first and both of mine just barely bounced out. Chris bit his lip and threw his next shot. It hit a cup, hopped up and landed right in a cup. He threw his arms into the air. "And he is still the champ!"

That was my line from wrestling Dad, but Chris beat me fair and square. All the guys were cheering for me as I stood over the ice chest. I took a big breath and leaned over. When my nose touched the water, I stood back up. "It's cold!"

"A deal is a deal, Teddy."

I took another breath and stuck my head in the chest. I have never felt anything that cold in my life. After I yanked my head back out, they gave me a towel. I put my shirt back on and dried my hair some more. I got pats on the back for being a good sport. I had so much fun at the party and the wedding. Renee and Chris gave me gift certificates to Best Buy. I was so excited that I would be able to buy more PlayStation games.

Renee now lives in Boston and we talk on the phone sometimes. Mostly, we text back and forth, and I tell her all the time how much I miss her. When she comes back to Cincinnati to visit her family, our families always get together for dinner. I love her family like they are my own. When Renee learned I was batboy for the Reds, I think she was almost excited as I was.

Two years before Renee's wedding, I was in Lauren's wedding. That was the first time I walked Sue down the aisle. For that wedding the groomsmen wore tuxedos, and the wedding took place in the chapel at Summit Country Day. The bachelor party was in Pittsburgh, but Mom wouldn't let me go to that party. It was too far away, and Dad was working and couldn't take me. But I should have gone, because the Reds were in town for a game, and Mike Leake had a no-hitter against the Pirates. Mike and Lauren still live in Cincinnati and I see them all the time. They always invite me to come over and watch the Bengals games with them, and they always come to my birthday party. They even came to the night I was the batboy.

ONCE PROM WAS OVER, THERE WERE still a few weeks of school left. I couldn't believe that my high school days were almost over. Like I mentioned before, Boomer died my senior year. That was awful, but so much of my last year at Colerain had been so great, I didn't want it to end. I remember sitting with Mom and Dad at dinner one night talking about everything.

"I can't believe all that happened this year," Mom said.

"You? Me either," I told her. "I sure had fun."

"All your years in high school were pretty good, I think," Dad added.

And they were good. I had lettered in swimming, football, and baseball all four years. I was even given a Senior Superlative Award by my teachers. My classmates chose Carla Mahaney and me as the winners of the Most School Spirit Award. Not long ago, I saw Carla at a Reds game and gave her a big hug.

"I can't believe it's been so long," she said.

"Do you still have spirit?" I asked her.

"Yes, we do!" she said enthusiastically.

After she walked away, I thought about lots of things from high school.

I had mixed emotions during graduation week. Mom said it was called a "bittersweet" time. Just like when I left Mercy Montessori, it was sad to say goodbye to all my teachers and friends. I was even sadder to say goodbye to Coach Coombs, Coach Newton, and Coach Jenke. I also said goodbye to Vince and Dominick, who were juniors at the time. I knew I would see them next year when I came back to help out on the team, but I knew things would never be the same. We would all go on our paths. Many would travel a long way and some would stay close to home. Most of my friends had a clue about what they wanted to do with their lives. I didn't know what the future held for me, but I did know it would be in Cincinnati.

THERE WERE SO MANY PEOPLE WHO helped me when I had bad days or cheered with me on good days. There's a big list of those people. Sean, Dominick, and Vince helped make me a better coach; the players on the team listened when I told them "way to go" or "don't give up." Renee made me feel all grown up when she went to the prom. For years, Mom and Dad told me I could fly to the moon.

Now I finally knew what they meant. I could be myself and still fit in. I could be on the swim team and sit in a regular class and laugh with other kids at lunch and go to a prom.

During the week of graduation I remember Mom sitting at dinner one night saying to me, "You know, Teddy, some people never thought you would get to your last week of high school. They sure were wrong." Then Dad told me how proud he was of me. I always tried to do the right thing and treat everyone nicely. But I did have some difficult days in school. I let small things bother me too much, like dropping the mail or forgetting my homework. Sometimes I cried when our football team or baseball team lost. Mom and Dad always made me feel better though after we talked about my rough days.

The day of graduation, all of my family, including my aunts and uncles, were there. Even Sean came back to cheer us on. He had graduated two years before, but always came back to Colerain to support the graduates. He put his arm around me and said, "Thanks for all you have done for me, Teddy."

"What do you mean?" I asked.

"Ever since I met you, Teddy, I never wanted to let you down. I'm a better person for having met you."

I didn't know what to say, so I just gave him a hug.

Graduation was in Millett Hall at Miami University. I was very nervous as I stood in line with the rest of the graduating seniors. When it was my time to walk up the stairs of the stage, I turned around and gave my family the thumbs-up sign. My Dad probably had a fit, because he worried about the students acting appropriately at the ceremony. But I couldn't help myself. I was pumped. On the stage, Mrs. Heintz, our principal, handed me my diploma and the whole crowd cheered. I smiled as big as I could, and she gave me a hug. I hurried down the stairs and guess who was right there to shake my hand—my dad.

Since Dad had to work right after graduation, we didn't celebrate until a week later. That gave us time to plan a big party at our house. Both my grandmothers came to the party, and all the relatives from both sides of the family. My brother was there and so were all the Roedersheimers. But the biggest surprise was that Sister Martha, Sister Aloyse, and Patty came to my graduation party. I was so excited that I threw my arms around all of them. Mom was afraid I was going to knock them over, since they all are so little, especially Sister Martha. Strange, they looked so tall when I was in the elementary grades.

I got some really cool gifts for graduation, including lots of sports video games. Everybody knows how much I love playing those kinds of games.

Once the party was over and everyone went home, my life felt different. It was time to grow up, but I was scared. I was really happy during my high school years, and I didn't want them to end. I knew I would really miss high school, but I would always be a Cardinal.

I didn't know what the future would be like without the routine of school. What does it mean to be a grown up? Do I have to get a job right away? Who would be my friends? Would I be lonely? The one thing I did know was that I was asked to stay on as coach for Colerain football. That made me very excited.

Chapter 14

BEFORE I GRADUATED FROM HIGH SCHOOL, MY PARENTS STARTED to research a program called Project SEARCH. We attended many meetings, and learned that Project SEARCH was developed at Cincinnati Children's Hospital Medical Center to train people with disabilities for all sorts of jobs. I learned online that the group has grown from a single program site at Cincinnati Children's to over 300 sites across the United States and Canada, England, Scotland, Ireland, and Australia. I really liked the people I met at these meetings, and Dad helped me fill out an application.

I found out in August after my senior year that I was accepted into Project SEARCH. I was a little nervous because football two-a-days had already started, and I was worried that I would be not able to handle it all. But Dad said I needed to make it work. After all, the instructors teach all kinds of job readiness skills, like how to dress for an interview and how to interact with people in the business world. They also teach you how to take the bus to work.

"But what if I'm not ready?"

"The people at Project SEARCH are there to help you," Dad said. "Your mom and I think it's a good idea. Besides, you have a month before the program starts."

It turned out that training at Project SEARCH was like school, even though the program took place at the PNC building downtown. The program was created for people with special needs who want to learn skills they can use in the work force. We would have a short class each morning with our teachers and then we were off to our internship for the rest of the day. I was in the program for a year. Every three months I would switch to a different job. My first internship was at PNC bank, one floor down from Project SEARCH's classroom area.

On my first day of work, a very nice lady named Lisa came out to the house to train me on catching the bus. She said she would take over once Mom drove me to the bus stop. She showed me how much the bus would cost and said, "Now make sure you have the right amount when your Mom drops you off." Then she made me show her the correct coins. We waited for the bus and soon it came around the corner. Once on the bus, Lisa showed me where to put my money. So, I counted out the correct change carefully, and then slid it in the metal slot. "Way to go, Teddy!" she said. "You'll be ready to ride by yourself in no time."

For the first few weeks, Lisa rode the bus with me to and from work. She wanted to make sure that when the time came, I could get to work and back home by myself. I sometimes became confused on the way home. I didn't catch the bus the same place I got off in the morning. Lisa would then take me to the right spot and after a few times I had no more problems. When the day came for me to go to work by myself, Dad rode the bus with me. I introduced him to the driver and my bus friends.

"It seems my son can make friends anywhere," Dad told the driver.

"I think you're right about that," the driver said. "We will look after him."

Someone in the back yelled, "We love Teddy!"

Once I was at work, Dad had Mom pick him up from downtown. I have been riding the bus by myself ever since.

AS AN INTERN AT THE PNC building, I had to have my own phone and memorize the address in case I got lost. I practiced over and over. "Excuse me," I practiced saying. "Do you know how to get to

4th and Vine?" Once there, I would sort mail or file papers in a large cabinet. I was used to sorting mail and filing, because that's what I did in the office at Colerain. I think everyone was surprised at how fast I could work. I finished work everyday at 2:10 and then I took the elevator up to Project SEARCH, checked out, and caught the bus at 2:30. I would get back to Northgate Mall about 3:15. Mom would pick me up and then drop me off at Colerain High School, so I could help Coach Newton with the football team. Mom then would drive back to her classroom at Houston Elementary to prepare for her next day of school.

Because of my work schedule, I was able to get to football practices on time, and I always showed up for night games in my 12th-man jersey. I never missed a game, not even the away games. We had an even better team in 2004 because of our new quarterback, Dominick Goodman. He was on the team his first years at Colerain as a running back. His senior year he took over as quarterback. And he was amazing. I didn't know him very well before that year, but I did see him at practice, and sometimes we would say "hey" in the halls. My mom had him in second grade for some of his subjects. On the field he made us a championship team. And even though we never talked about it, I think he told the other players not to say mean things to me. Sometimes a few players would laugh at me when I walked into the locker room, and Dominick would give them a look, and they would stop right away. Other players would act like I didn't belong, but Dominick never made me feel like that. He was always great to me.

One day at practice, Dominick took a break while the backup quarterback went on the field. He walked up to me and patted my shoulder. "I watch how you are Teddy. I know you want us to win."

I smiled and told him, "I sure do. It drives me crazy and makes me really sad when we lose."

"Well, I'm gonna see what I can do about that." He smiled and the coach yelled for him to get back out on the field. As he headed for the huddle, he turned and said, "You just watch." He meant what he said because we had the best season ever at Colerain.

If Coach got mad, I got mad. But as the season went on, Coach got mad less and less. We kept making first downs and getting touchdowns. I would run down the field and give the first down signal with the referee. If we scored, I would jump up and down and yell, "Touchdown!" When Dominick would score, he would come right over to me and we would bump our fists together before he went to the bench. He did that after each touchdown. By the time we played our biggest rival at the end of the season, we had not lost a game. It was so much fun to be happy after every game.

THEN WE WENT TO THE STATE playoffs! We won the first four games. We were playing so well that we outscored the other teams 141-12. Dad said the students and teachers were going crazy all week. The only thing they talked about was the game. I even had trouble concentrating at Project SEARCH. At practice, Coach Newton and the other coaches told the team to just "keep doing what you've been doing." Dominick and the other players tried to stay calm, but we were all excited. Mom and Dad would ask me how the team looked at practice, and I would tell them the same thing every day. "We're ready!"

Then it was time for the championship game. We played in Canton, Ohio, where the Pro Football Hall of Fame is. The team we were playing was from Canton. It was like a home game for them. When we ran onto the field, I couldn't believe how many people were there. The stands were crammed with fans. That made us even more nervous. And it was really cold. Then it was time to play and the referee tossed the coin. We won the toss but the game started out bad. Dominick fumbled three times, and we weren't playing too good. Dominick banged his helmet on the bench and yelled at himself after his last fumble. Coach was upset and I paced up and down the sidelines. It was not looking like we would win. I saw Dominick standing by Coach, and I went over and stood next to him. "You remember what you said?" I asked Dominick. "Way back in practice?" I might not be good at math and some other things, but I have a really good memory. I remembered what he told me. So when Dominick didn't answer, I said, "You said you wouldn't let us lose, remember? You said, 'I'm gonna see what I can do about that.'"

I waited on him. Then Dominick smiled and patted me on the back. "Yes I did, Teddy." Right after that we got the ball back. We were losing 10-6 when Dominick and the offense ran on the field. A few plays later Dominick ran for a touchdown. Then we scored again and again. We had a really good running back named Mister Simpson and he ran all over the field. What a cool name—Mister. By the end of the game we had scored 50 points to the other team's 10. Dominick actually set a record of running the ball in a football championship. He did what he said he would do. As the clock ran out, all the coaches and players and a bunch of fans ran out onto the field. I was so excited! All of the Colerain players jumped into a big pile, and pulled me into the center of them. The Colerain fans were going wild, and my voice became hoarse from yelling, "We are the champions!" I will never forget that season, the year we won the state championship.

We had a reunion of the team in 2014, and it was so much fun to see the players again. Some looked older and some hadn't changed much. The biggest change was that all the players gave me big hugs and seemed very glad to see me. Vince Forcillini said he was my biggest fan. "I never think of my high school years without thinking of you, Teddy. You were a great example to us all."

I need to tell you about Vince. He was the starting tackle on the football team his senior year. People said he was the fastest lineman on the team. Besides being fast, he was an awesome player, and one of the reasons we won state in 2004.

One day towards the end of my senior year, Mom told me that someone had written a poem about me.

"Me? Why?"

"I think he wanted to."

"What kind of poem?"

Mom smiled, "Does it matter, Teddy?"

I told her it didn't, and then I asked her, "Who wrote it?"

"Well, from what I understand, it was Vince."

Apparently, Vince had to write a poem for his English class about someone who inspired him. And he chose me. I learned that his teacher had showed the poem to my dad. Dad thought it was really cool and asked Vince if he could have a copy of the poem. He brought it home for me the next day.

I read the first half of the poem, and it made me feel great and sad at the same time. Vince wrote about how I brought the most spirit to the team. He also mentioned that I didn't let it bother me when the players said mean things about me, or when they make fun of me. It did bother me, but not for more than a day. My dad told me that if a bully knows he gets to you, he would never stop. Some of the words in the poem made me sad. After I read the poem, Mom asked me if there was something wrong.

"I'm okay, Mom," I told her. "I'm okay."

Mom knew better than to say anything else. She knows I don't like to talk about sad feelings.

In the second part of the poem, Vince said I was a hero. Wow. A hero. I always thought heroes saved lives and were firemen and policemen and teachers. But Vince said I was his hero. We still keep in contact, and every time I see him, I remind him of how much I loved that poem. He titled his poem "Cheerleader."

Cheerleader

His handicap might slow him down,
But he will never frown
Bringing school spirit and lots of cheer
The team will have nothing to fear,
Oblivious to the mocking and jeering
He continues with his cheering,
Inspiring all who see
He wills the team to victory,
Although this hero of mine will never play
He cheers every Friday

This hero doesn't boast
This hero is different than most,
While he is shouting for his team
People like him can only dream,
Dream of being a hero in every way
I wish we all could be like him.
Every day

By Vincent Forcellini
Grade 12

Teddy (age 16) at Meet the Team night, freshman year

Teddy (age 17), Family, and Mimi and Papa, Christmas

Teddy (age 17) in Hawaii, 2000

Teddy (age 18) diving in the pool

Teddy (age 19) leading the team on to the field

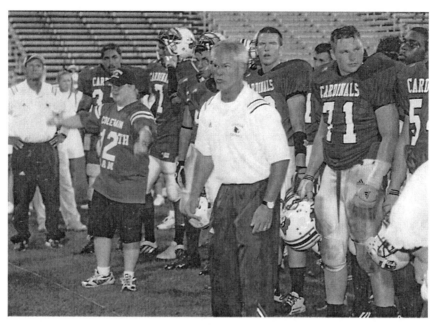

Teddy (age 20) with the Team and Kerry Coombs at Regionals

Teddy (age 20) with cheerleaders

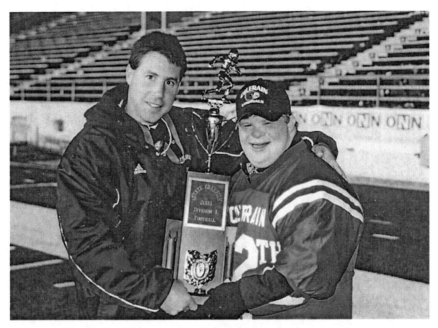

Coach Newton, Teddy (age 21) with the State trophy

David, Erin, and Teddy (age 21), prom night

Teddy (age 21) on the sidline at State Championships

Teddy (age 21) and Dominick Goodman

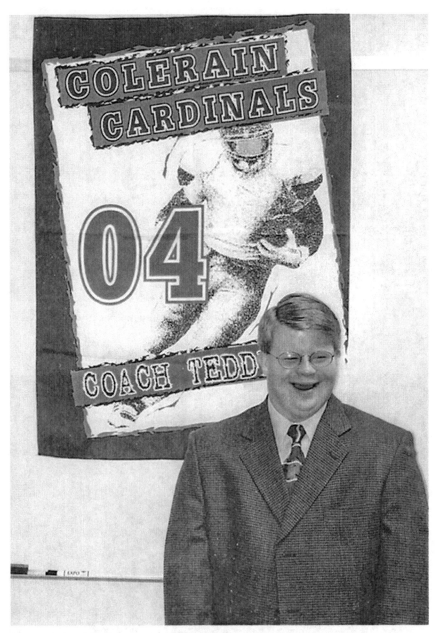

Teddy (age 21) in front of the senior recognition flag

Teddy (age 21) and Vince Forcillini

Teddy (age 21) and Renee, prom night

Teddy (age 21) and Dad, graduation night 2004

Teddy (age 21) at graduation with friends Rachel and Tyler

At the Unified Softball Team Championship,
Teddy won the game with a walk-off hit.

Chapter 15

AFTER THREE MONTHS AT PNC, I WENT TO WORK AT THE Hamilton County Courthouse. It was nine blocks away from Project SEARCH, which is more than I like to walk. Also, it was wintertime and it was cold! I could see my breath every time I took a step. I had a job coach at Project SEARCH named Shirlene Gilb. She would go to each of my internships with me at first and show me how to do the job, so the people who worked at the various places wouldn't have to stop their work and help me. As I spent more time at the different jobs, she would come with me less and less.

In the mornings Mom would ask, "Teddy, do you have your gloves and hat? It's cold out there."

"Yes, Mom. I know it's cold."

She would take me to the bus stop and usually wait until the bus showed up. Once downtown I would exit the bus and walk immediately to Starbucks to buy a chocolate milk. That made my walk to the courthouse more fun, even though the milk was cold. My job at the courthouse was to file folders after the lawyers were done with them. The room where I worked had long shelves full of folders. I filed each folder by its color and number. Most of the folders held what's called civil cases. Sometimes I would put a file back on the shelf and make that sound you hear every time they change scenes on *Law and Order*. "Dunk! Dunk!" Everyone around me would laugh. I had some good times at the Courthouse.

Somehow I survived the cold winter. My next rotation was in the mailroom at Fifth Third Bank. It was way out in Madisonville, the bank's main office, so I had to catch a couple of different buses. When I walked in there for the first time, I couldn't believe how much mail there was. Mitch Morgan, Development Program Manager, told me that Fifth Third Bank receives and sends out so much mail that it has its own zip code. That's a lot of mail! It was my job to help make sure it all got to where it needed to go. I made some good friends in the mailroom. Even though the bus ride was longer, I would have been happy to keep working there. But unfortunately, they didn't have a place for me when I finished my three-month internship. Mitch told me that Fifth Third Bank likes having people with special needs work for them. He says that we don't change jobs as often as other people. "I can depend on you, Teddy," he said. "I always know you're going to do your job. That's a great thing for a business."

After my year of training was finished, I hoped to get a real job. I loved working, and I was excited about making my own money. Then I could spend it on whatever I wanted.

"When I get hired," I told Dad, "maybe I can save up and buy season tickets to the Reds games."

"Well, maybe. You never know."

"Or maybe I'll just buy some CDs and video games, or go to Taco Bell," I said.

"I am sure you'll be able to buy some with your check," Dad answered. "Maybe you can buy an organizer for your closet."

I smiled at that. "I don't think so."

One day, Shirlene called and said they had a job for me. A real job! It was at Hillcrest Training School. I was so excited!

After I calmed down, I asked Dad, "What's Hillcrest?"

"Well, it's a place where teenagers go when they get in trouble."

"Like talking back to the teacher? Or worse?"

Dad said, "Yeah, worse than that. Some of them have committed crimes like robbery or injuring someone."

I thought about that and wondered if I would be okay there.

Dad thought the same thing. "I'll take you out there, and we'll talk to some of the people before you commit."

The center was like its own little town. The buildings were spread over seventy acres, at least that's what Dad said. Dad took me to the superintendent's office. I was sure glad to be in there as a visitor.

Dad talked to the superintendent for a while and they agreed that I would only do work in the office building. If I ever needed to go anywhere else, someone would have to go with me.

The superintendent told Dad, "We'll make sure Teddy is safe. He'll be near my office just about all day."

"When can I start?" I asked him.

"Next week is fine."

I raised a fist. "Yes!"

"You'll be working Mondays, Tuesdays, and Thursdays."

"When do I get paid?" I asked. I already had my CDs and video games picked out.

"Twice a month, just like everybody else." He smiled and we shook hands.

My first week of work was very exciting. I became friends with the ten people working in the offices. I was given jobs filing papers, scanning letters, and entering data. Sometimes I would even shred papers. Pam Wilson was my supervisor, and she was the one who showed me everything I needed to learn and do at Hillcrest. I even had my own office and phone. But to tell the truth, I really liked working in Pam's office. We talked about sports and her grandchildren when we had a break. She was so nice. She was the business manager for Hillcrest and purchased everything for the office and school. I would help her because we had to keep really good records for the Hamilton County Courts. One day Shirlene came out to see how I was doing. She noticed that I was putting one paper at a time in the shredder. "You're going to take forever to finish," she said. "You need to put four or five pieces of paper in at a time."

Even though I worked at a place for young people who had done some bad things, I never really talked to any of them. I would see them around the campus, but I stayed with my co-workers and made sure to never wander off. Lots of the students looked like kids I went to high school with, but others looked pretty tough.

On my days off, I would stay at home and do chores. If it was winter, I might shovel snow or clean up my room. And maybe my closet. The rest of the year I would sweep, dust, and take out the trash. Stuff like that. My chores came after reading the sports section of the *Cincinnati Enquirer* and watching *Sports Center* on ESPN. I always DVR'd the games and watched them again the next day. If the Reds or Bengals were playing, I would read all I could about them in the paper.

People at Hillcrest knew they could ask me anything about Cincinnati sports and I would know it. Many times they would ask, "Teddy, when are the Reds in town again? I might take my kids to the game." Often my co-workers asked about the games from the day before. If I watched *Sports Center* that morning, I would tell them the statistics for all the teams. Reds or Bengals, I had a head for sports.

I ended up working at Hillcrest for nine years and really loved my job and the people there. But things started to change at Hillcrest. A private company bought Hillcrest, and then made the decision to downsize. Many people lost their jobs, but I was one of the lucky ones. I kept my job. But things were not the same. There wasn't as much for me to do and I became very bored.

When Shirlene came to check on me, she seemed worried. "I'm still trying to get you on at Fifth Third Bank," she said. "You don't seem as happy here as you used to be." About that same time I became the batboy for the Reds, and my story played on ESPN. After that, my co-workers high-fived me every time I came into the office. The company even put me on their website. I still wished I had more to do.

OUTSIDE OF WORK, THOUGH, MY LIFE couldn't get more exciting. After I was the bat boy for the first time, but before the *E:60* special, John Boehner, the Speaker of the House at that time, invited my parents and me to Washington, D.C. His office called the Reds and invited us to The State of the Union Address. They asked Rick Stowe, the equipment manager, and his son Luke, the batboy for the Reds, to go too, but they couldn't go because it was the same time as spring training.

They invited John Erardi, the reporter who wrote the article about my night as batboy with the Reds. They also offered a ticket to Jeff Swinger, the photographer who took all the pictures in the dugout, including the photograph with Brandon Phillips smiling at me.

Later, when speaking to the staff in Speaker Boehner's office, my mom asked if there would be room for David and Erin to go. They were able to work it out so they could attend the State of the Union Address with us. I was thrilled they were going!

"Are we really going to go?" I asked Mom and Dad when they first told me about it.

Mom and Dad thought about it for a couple of seconds, then Mom said, "I'll have to take time off from work. But yes, Teddy, we are going!"

I jumped up and down with my arms in the air. "Yes, yes!"

So a few days before President Obama's speech, we packed up and flew to Washington, D.C. On the plane I sat with Jeff Swinger, who was more like a big brother than a grown-up. As we flew into the city, we could see the Washington Monument. "Jeff! Look at this! The Washington Monument!" I shouted.

"Look just past it, Teddy, and you can see Congress," Jeff said. "That's where we'll be in two nights."

As I climbed down the stairs of the plane, I felt just like the President getting off Air Force One. In the airport, we picked up our rental car. It was Sunday afternoon. We arrived in Washington early so we could enjoy the tours that Speaker Boehner's staff arranged. After lunch at a great Mexican restaurant where I had quesadillas with extra salsa, we decided to drive out to Arlington Cemetery.

Once we reached Arlington, I was amazed when I saw all the white grave markers. They went up and down the hill for a long way. Dad said that each of them was for a soldier who died fighting for our country and that many of them were not even as old as I was. It made me sad to see all the graves. Then we went to visit President Kennedy's grave. He died before I was born, but I knew all about him from Sister Aloyse's class. On his grave is a burning flame that never goes out.

After that we went to the Tomb of the Unknown Soldier. Dad said lots of soldiers died in wars and their family never had a body to bring home.

Mom said, "That's why our country built this monument, Teddy, to honor their courage. We never want to forget what they did." It makes me sad to think of moms and dads who don't get to say goodbye to their children. There was a soldier marching back and forth in front of the grave. We watched the Changing of the Guard. All the people around us were very quiet. Some of the spectators were crying; I felt very bad for them. The Changing of the Guard really made me proud of my country. Later when we were walking back to the car, I talked to Jeff about it.

Jeff asked, "Teddy, do you think you can march that way?"

I immediately said, "Yes!" and marched just like I had seen the soldier march. I wanted to be very respectful as I did it. John Erardi even marched with me. "Heel to toe. Heel to toe. Walk." We both repeated these words as we advanced down the path of Arlington Cemetery.

After walking all over Arlington, we checked into our hotel and then had a relaxing dinner at McCormick and Schmidt's. Back at the hotel, Jeff talked me into getting some Oreo cookies out of the vending machine. We sat in the lobby eating our cookies until

Mom insisted we call it a night. We had to get up early in the morning for our scheduled tours.

On Monday, we took a tour of the Capitol and many of the important buildings in Washington, D.C.. My favorite place was the National Archives Building. The curator showed us famous documents signed by Lincoln and Washington. She brought out a draft of the Gettysburg Address and was surprised that I recognized it immediately. The heading on the paper said the "Executive House." The curator asked if anyone knew what the Executive House was now called, and I immediately answered, "The White House!"

Then she pulled out more documents to show us, and before she could tell us what they were, I would finish her sentence. I think she was shocked at how many documents I knew. Even Mom and Dad and Jeff and John were looking at me like *how do you know that?* But I like history and I remembered all the things Sister Aloyse talked about in history class at Mercy Montessori. We then left the National Archives Building and went to the Supreme Court, and then back to Speaker Boehner's office.

When we arrived at the Capitol Building, we had to go through security. Of course, my mom set off all the alarms. She does this at all the airports and everywhere there are metal detectors. Mom has two replaced knees and a replaced hip, so she always has to step aside and be checked by security guards.

Finally, we went to Speaker Boehner's office. He was in a committee meeting so we met his administrative assistant, Amy, and the Speaker's other assistants, Tommy and John. While I was in the office, I sat in Speaker Boehner's chair and held his gavels. His desk was very small, much smaller than my dad's desk that he has in his home office. Yet the Speaker's desk was placed in front of a window with a perfect view of the Washington Monument. Amy told us that the Speaker always wanted to be reminded of why he was in Washington.

After we left Boehner's office, I saw something really amazing. In the middle of the Capitol is a big round dome called the Rotunda. We stood under it and looked up at the ceiling, with all the other tourists. There are paintings on the ceiling, but they are way up high so it's hard to tell what each one is. Tommy was showing us around and suggested, "Why don't we get a closer look?"

"That would be great," I told him. "How?"

"Let's go to the top of the dome. But you have to climb some stairs."

"Yes!" I said with a grin. "I don't really like to climb stairs, but this time I'll do it."

My mom said she would wait in the Speaker's office with Amy. "With my knees it would take until tomorrow to climb all those steps!"

Tommy took us up many, many, many steps to a door that opened to a catwalk. Once we were inside the dome, we looked down to the floor below us. It was a long way down; I was me a little scared. People were looking up at us and waving. Then Tommy told us that the original roof of the Rotunda was right above us. We walked around the railing and went through another door that led to a narrow passageway with steps. My Dad and Jeff barely fit through the opening, but managed somehow to get up the steps.

At the top, Tommy opened the door to the roof of the Capitol! John Erardi had to duck to get through, but once we were outside, we could see all of Washington, D.C. from up there. I was amazed at how many streets and cars were in the city. It was very windy on the top of the Capitol, and we had to hold onto the railing. Tommy told us that not many people get to go up to the top of the Rotunda. "But we were told that Teddy deserved this for all he's done for Cincinnati," he said to John and Jeff.

That made my dad smile. And it made me very happy. I didn't know that I did anything special for Cincinnati. I was just being me.

And this was not the end of the day. We still had more to do and see.

That evening, all of us were invited to dinner given by the National Down Syndrome Congress. While we were at the Italian restaurant, Representative Michele Bachman came over to the table. She wanted to talk to my family because she supports legislation, like the ABLE Act, which helps special needs people save money. Representative Bachman even had me come over to her separate dinner meeting that she was attending to meet other members of Congress. Congress has since passed the ABLE Act, but it is up to each state to decide how to use it.

On Tuesday morning, we had a tour of the White House. My brother, David, flew in from South Bend that morning and met us at the White House. Erin, my sister-in-law (but I just call her my sister), was flying in later from her consulting meeting in Tennessee.

Later in the day we were invited to a reception in the Capitol to have a private meeting with Speaker Boehner. But first we had to get there. Dad was in one cab with Jeff and John; David, Mom, and I were in the second cab. The other group made it to the Capitol without any problem. Their cab driver knew where he was going, but our cabbie had no clue. He tried to find the Capitol but got lost. David was on the phone with my dad, and he was going crazy trying to figure out how to get us there. Then the cab driver started using really bad words, and yelled, "This is why I don't come to D.C.!"

My brother said, "I thought you worked here. Can't you just look for it? It's a huge building with a white dome."

"I live in Baltimore!" he yelled. Then he made a quick turn down a street. I looked at all the cars coming at us and asked, "Isn't this a one way street?"

We turned at the next light. The whole time the cabbie was honking his horn and cursing. My brother was still on the phone with Dad, and my mom kept saying, "We are going to miss the whole thing! You have to get us there before they close the streets! The President is coming!"

It was so crazy; I didn't know what to do. "What time is it? What time is it?" I cried. "We are going to miss the State of the Union address!"

When we crossed Embassy Row, we knew we were in trouble. The cabbie kept punching his GPS, saying, "This is why I don't come to this city!"

After an hour, we got close enough to the Capitol to walk. "Let us out!" my mom demanded. "They are starting to close the roads." She then turned to David, "Just take Teddy and go. I'll be there as soon as I can."

We walked up a huge hill and finally made it to the Capitol. I saw Erin and Amy on the sidewalk out front and yelled their names. I gave Erin a big hug. We waited a minute for Mom, and then we all walked inside together.

We first went to John Boehner's office and met the rest of his staff.

Someone in his office asked, "How's your day been so far?"

My dad said, "Don't ask. It's great now."

Then Amy led me over to her desk, and asked me to sign the pictures of Brandon Phillips smiling at me that Jeff had sent to Speaker Boehner. Amy told me that I was to have a twenty-minute private meeting with the Speaker.

Then Speaker Boehner came in and we all walked into his private quarters. The Speaker talked with me about the Reds and my days as the batboy. He told me he was proud of me, and said, "You have done an amazing job, and you are very important to everyone in Cincinnati."

"Well, you're doing a good job too, Speaker Boehner," I said.

"Thank you, that means a lot to me, Teddy."

It was so exciting. Then the Speaker said he had something to give me. He handed me a baseball bat. But not just any old bat. This one was a special red bat that he had made just for me. The Speaker even had my name engraved on it. How cool is that?

I told the Speaker that I had something special for him. I gave him one of my Topps baseball cards with the picture of Dusty Baker and me. John Erardi gave the Speaker one of his books on the history of the Reds, and then we all sat down to talk about Cincinnati and what other things I was doing. After thirty-five minutes, one of his staffers came in and reminded him that his twenty minutes was up, and he was late for the next guest. Before we left, Speaker Boehner put my baseball card in his cabinet where he kept his gavel. He placed my card right next to his Moeller baseball hat from high school.

We then walked across the hall to the reception area where many important people, including the Joint Chiefs of Staff and their wives, were enjoying Cincinnati Skyline Chili, Graeter's Ice Cream, and Montgomery Inn barbecue.

Finally it was time to go to the State of the Union Address. We had to go through metal detectors, so we couldn't take our phones, cameras, or iPads. Jeff Swinger got to take his camera since he had a press pass. We sat in the Speaker's private box in the gallery, Row A. The wives of the Joint Chiefs of Staff sat behind us, and Mom was thrilled to see that Tony Bennett was seated directly behind them. Then the senators and congressmen from both sides came in and sat in their seats on the floor of the House. When they announced the President, it was thrilling. Before the President started speaking, he looked up at me and waved. I returned the wave, and then later I waved again as the President left the floor.

When we were about to leave, an aide for Senator Rubio came over to us and asked if we could wait around until Senator Rubio's response to the President's address was over. Not long after that Marco Rubio came up and said he had seen me on ABC news and wanted to have his picture taken with me. A senator. Wow. I was honored he knew who I was.

In the airport on the way home, we all had to go through the scanner and, of course, my mom set the alarm off so she had to through the full body machine. After the scan, while Mom was putting on her shoes, Tony Bennett stepped into the body scanner. She couldn't believe he was in line right behind her! Tony Bennett! It took a while for my mom to gather her belongings, so I waited for her. Then Tony Bennett came out of the scanner and looked straight at me. He smiled and said, "I remember you! I sat behind you at the State of the Union Address."

"Yes! You did!" I said. "My Mimi is going to be so happy that I met you! She loves you!"

Tony Bennett shook my hand and said, "Tell your Mimi that I send my love."

Overall, it was a wonderful experience. I still have my red bat in my room to remind me of my meeting with the Speaker. I will always remember the President waving at me, and how nice everyone in Washington was.

AFTER THE TRIP, I RESUMED MY life of working three days a week at Hillcrest, swimming, and pursuing my latest hobby, ballroom dancing. One day at work, Shirlene called and asked if I would like to talk to golfers at a fund-raising tournament at King's Island. I don't know much about golf. I have played putt-putt and I have watched my brother play but that's about all I know. When they asked me to speak, I thought, "Why me?" Then Shirlene said they wanted me to speak about Project SEARCH.

"I can do that," I said.

"Well, I am sure everyone will be thrilled to meet you," she told me.

The purpose of the golf tournament was to raise money for Project SEARCH. I was to speak at the dinner afterwards. Mom helped me write out my speech, and when the time came, I was ready.

"Project SEARCH has made my life better," I told the golfers. "If I had not met Shirlene and everyone else who took the time to show me how to be a better worker, I don't know where I would be today. They taught me how to ride the bus and to find my way around Cincinnati." All of the people were smiling as I spoke. "And as much as it has helped me, I know there are lots of special needs people out there who could use the same lucky break I got when Dad found Project SEARCH." I also told them how it has helped lots of people with disabilities get jobs and learn how to be on their own. "If Project SEARCH is not in every city, it should be."

Shirlene and Mitch Morgan were sitting near the podium and after my speech I gave them a big hug. The golfers applauded and lots of them wanted to talk to me.

A YEAR LATER, SHIRLENE CALLED MOM and Dad saying she might have a job opening at Madisonville in the Fifth Third Bank mailroom.

"Would you like to give it a try?" Mom asked me.

"I really liked it there and the people were great."

"It's been ten years, Teddy, since you interned there. Most of those folks are probably somewhere else."

I nodded and said, "Okay, but can I try anyway?"

The next day, Dad took me down to Fifth Third Bank for an interview with Shirlene.

"So, you would like to work here at Fifth Third?" she asked me.

I smiled real big. "That would be great!"

"Well, I asked around and some of the people you worked with ten years ago are still here. You know what they told me, Teddy?"

"Is it about my job?" I asked.

She smiled and said, "They said that working with you made

169

them want to come to work. When I told them you might be coming back, they couldn't have been more thrilled."

"Wow. Really?"

"So, if you want the job, it's yours." Shirlene shook my hand. "Welcome back to Fifth Third."

I was so excited, but I worried about telling everybody at Hillcrest. I knew the people there would be sad that I was leaving, especially Pam. I had worked with her for nine years, and we were really close. It would be hard to give my two weeks notice, but I knew Fifth Third was the right place for me.

Now I am back at Fifth Third where I work in the mailroom two days a week. I thought there was lots of mail when I was an intern, but there are mountains of it now. I get up at six, read the paper, eat something good for breakfast (burrito!) and then go to work. Because my hours are 7:30 to 3:30, I can work a second job at the Fans Accommodation Booth at The Great American Ballpark whenever the Reds are in town. When the Reds have a day game and I'm scheduled to work at the bank, Fifth Third lets me switch my days. Another really cool thing about Fifth Third is that I am not the only person with special needs who works there. Actually I have helped train many special people like me.

Fifth Third and the Reds have figured out what good employees we are. I wish more businesses would hire people with special needs. It is really hard for us to find a job. For those of us who can, we want to get up and ride the bus and be on time and all that goes with having a job. Maybe it will get better for my friends who look for a job and get told no over and over. I sure hope so. All of us need support.

Chapter 16

I haven't told you much about my older brother, David. He is a very special person to me and I love him very much. He and his wife, Erin, live in South Bend with their two sons. David works in sales for AFLAC, the company with the big white duck! South Bend is where Notre Dame is, which is pretty neat because we have always been Fighting Irish fans. David's the only person in all my family of cousins, aunts, and uncles who doesn't live in Cincinnati. When we go up to South Bend to visit, I love hanging out with my brother and his family. His kids are super fun and we play all kinds of video games. Sports games are our favorite. When David left to go to college, I really missed him. I think he missed me, too. When he got the job in South Bend, we started either talking on the phone or texting each other every day. Out of the two, I am not much for talking on the phone. I sort of say what I need to say and then go back to what I was doing. But I can text all day long!

When David was in middle school and high school, we went to all of his games. He played everything: football, baseball, basketball, and soccer. I loved watching him run around on the field and court, but the noise at his games really bothered me. I would cover my ears or wear two ski hats. Now kids wear earphones to drown out the noise. I really wish I'd had some back then.

David was bigger than most of the other boys his age, so he played on the line in football. Usually he played guard, but sometimes he played center or tackle. I asked him one time what really happens on the field, since it's hard to see what's going on down there from the stands. "Do you just bump into the other guy and then fall down?" It sure looked like that to me.

"No! There's all kind of things going on. It's where all the action is. The running backs try not to get hit. I open holes for the running backs. I also protect the quarterbacks just like I protect you." He balled up his fist and smacked it into his palm. "But, getting hit and hitting someone else is what I do. Those of us who play on the line love it."

Before he was in high school, he would come home from practice very dirty and mom would take his uniform and wash it as soon as he got home. She said it was so "the stains don't have time to set." She wouldn't let him in the house with his uniform on, so he had to take it off in the garage. Then he would run to the bathroom to shower. "It's cold!" he would complain.

"Some tough guy you are," my mom told him as he ran to the bathroom.

He got so good at football that the Colerain high school coaches came to watch him play one day when he was in the 8th grade. Dad was excited about that and he told Mom, "They want to see when he might be ready for varsity ball." During the game, I walked over to the coaches and told them that number 55 was my brother. I'm sure they already knew that since my dad worked at the school, and I had met the coaches several times. But I was so proud of David that I talked about him whenever I got the chance. I would tell anybody who would listen, "My brother is out there and he's really good."

It turned out he was ready for Varsity in the 10th grade. He still played guard and was one of the toughest players on the team. By the time he was a senior, he was the offensive team captain. It was exciting to watch him lead his team through the banner before games. Sometimes I would see him sneak a quick look up to our seats. I remember when he gave me a thumbs up while he was by the bench getting water. Who would've thought that a few years later I would be running through the Colerain football banner?

He also played basketball all four years and was captain his senior year. Since he was one of the biggest players, the coach put him at center. The team made it to the region finals his senior year, but his football team made it all the way to the state finals that year.

When David was a junior, he quit baseball. He loved the game, but he loved his family more. That year, Dad found out that he had colon cancer. He had to have radiation treatments and chemotherapy after dealing with middle school kids all day. Mom would pick him up and take him to the hospital five days a week. That meant there was no one at home to take care of me after I got off the Mercy Montessori bus. At first Mimi and Papa came over to the house, but then David decided he should be the one to take care of me after school because it was too hard on Mimi and Papa. Sometimes Mom and Dad didn't get home until after seven.

By the next football season, Dad was better and in remission, and while David didn't go back to baseball, he did pick another sport—throwing the discus. As David always does, he was good enough to qualify for state.

Once he finished high school, David played football at Butler University. David earned grants to help my parents with the cost of his tuition. But things were still tough for my parents. They now had the added expense of college along with my tuition at Mercy. But my parents were okay with that. "That's what parents do for their kids," Mom told me.

David was so excited when he found out that he had made Butler's football team. We all were! If he had been going to a school far away, I would've been really sad. Thank goodness, Butler is in Indianapolis, only an hour and a half away. It almost takes that long to make it down to a Reds or Bengals game when there's lots of traffic.

I asked David one day, "Are you going to sleep in the Hinkle Fieldhouse with all the football players?"

"No, Teddy, I'm going to sleep in Ross Hall. That's a dorm where the freshmen live."

"What's a dorm?"

"It's like a big hotel, but the rooms are filled with eighteen-year-olds."

"Will you keep your doors open all the time, like we do when we travel with our friends?"

"Only if the girls come over!"

I started laughing, but Mom didn't think that was funny. "David! Not in front of Teddy. You know big-mouth will repeat it to Mimi and Papa!"

David played offensive guard at Butler just like in middle school and high school. I am sure he still enjoyed blocking and protecting, but sometimes the opposing players would hit him really hard. Some of those guys weighed a ton and if they fell on you, it could hurt. I wouldn't want any of them falling on me. If that were me, I'd yell, "Get off of me!" I'm not small, but I don't do well with pain. I couldn't stand to watch it when David got hit. Sometimes I had to cover my eyes.

We went to all of David's home and away games. Most of the games were in the Midwest, but we did watch him play in San Diego, Dallas, and Richmond. The only game we didn't go to was the one he played in Cologne, Germany. That is Indianapolis's sister city, and David's team played the semi-professional Cologne Crocodiles. David's team spent a week in Germany and saw lots of famous historical sites and castles. I sure wish I could have gone. I love history, especially ancient history.

David played football all four years at Butler. My parents and I had special seats for the Butler football games. We sat in the Touchdown Club, a covered area near the end zone. It was a great place because we had a great view of the players as they kicked extra points and field goals. I love the name because I always wanted the Bulldogs to make touchdowns! Coach LaRose, the head football coach, always arranged for food to be brought in for us. The caterers served hot dogs, hamburgers, barbeque, and even my favorite chili. I would get my food and go to my special place on a landing just under the Touchdown Club. I wanted to be away from all the cheering because the noise hurt my ears. The sound goes right through my eardrums because I've had so many sets of tubes in my ears.

There were steps on the landing that led down to the medical room where the players were treated for injuries. The landing was the best place to sit and see the whole field. I could watch the plays being called in from the sidelines. I would yell, "Run" if the other team's quarterback handed off. When we had the ball, I would yell at David, "Make that block!" I knew he heard me because sometimes he looked over at me.

One time David went to the medical room instead of going to the locker room inside Hinkle Hall. I knew something was wrong, so I slipped down to the medical room to see what was wrong. When I peeked in the window, I could see David getting an IV in his arm. A needle! I hate needles! I ran back up to tell my dad and mom. They said David was probably dehydrated from the heat and playing so hard. Dad said, "Remember, Teddy, that happens to you when you get sick." So I went back to my special place. David came out at the end of half time and gave me a thumbs up. Whew! I was really glad.

SOME OF THE GAMES WE WENT to were in November and December, so it was cold. I remember David's last game. It was November of 1999, and it was really cold. I couldn't stop drinking hot chocolate and then I needed to go to the bathroom. The game had a minute to go and we were about to win. All we needed was a field goal. Then our team called a timeout. And then I *really* had to go. I told mom, "If I can't go right now, I don't think I can make it."

Dad jumped in, "But we're about to win!"

My brother was the long snapper for the team and there was no way I was leaving. He was all lined up ready to hike the ball to the field goal kicker, and then the other team called a timeout. Augh! I ran quickly up the steps to the Touchdown Club restroom, did what I had to do, and hurried back to my special place just in time to see David snap the ball. The kicker made the field goal and Butler won.

I WAS SAD WHEN DAVID GRADUATED from Butler, because our football days, we thought, were over. David did stay at Butler as a graduate assistant and helped coach the team. That year I was a freshman in high school, and I was helping coach our football team. Our weekends were filled with Colerain games on Friday, Butler games on Saturday, and the Bengals on Sunday. I think my parents were "footballed" out, but I never was. I was always ready for Monday Colerain football practices.

After David started college, my Mimi and Papa started taking our whole family on trips to Hawaii. They took all their kids and grandkids, not just our family. My mom's brother, Uncle Eddie, and his wife, Aunt Caryl, went on the trip. And of course, my cousins Alissa, Kristin, and Eddie III came along. I loved those trips! We went from the time I was in junior high until I was a freshman in high school. The last time we went was the summer before 9/11. We didn't go any more after that because my Papa passed away. My Papa loved those trips and he loved to make his family happy.

One year my Papa invited my Mimi-Over-the-River to go with us. Mimi Kremer, my dad's mother, lived in Fort Thomas, Kentucky. We had to cross the Ohio River to reach her house, so that's why we called her Mimi-Over-the-River. We always sang "Over the River and Through the Woods" as we drove over the bridge that connects Ohio to Kentucky. My Papa Kremer died when I was six years old, so he never went with us to Hawaii.

The plane ride to Hawaii was really long, especially for my grandparents. Maybe that's why they always booked us in first class. During the twelve-hour flight, I read the paper, played with my toy wrestlers, and stared out the window. I loved looking out at the clouds. My favorite time was at night. I would stay awake all night just to see the sun rise. Those sunrises were so beautiful. I would wake my mom and dad, and sometimes David, so they could see all the colors decorating the sky. They never were as excited as I was about the sunrise. I never had to wake my Mimi up though. She was always awake when I was. "I enjoy watching you as much as the sunrise, Teddy," she told me once. "You get so excited, you make me feel young again."

We always stayed in the Hawaiian Hilton on the island of Oahu. There were several different towers in the Hilton, and we always stayed in the Ali Tower. There was a pool on top of the tower, and it was really cool. The waiters and waitresses even brought us drinks when we were in the pool. One time I ordered a Diet Coke, and when Christie, our waitress, brought it to me, I gave her a tip and signed the bill just like everyone else did. Later, my Mimi checked the bill and asked, "Who in the world left a $5.00 tip for a $2.50 diet coke?"

"I did, of course!" I said. "I'm a great tipper."

"You sure are!" Mimi said laughing. "I think it's great that you left a tip. That's what you are supposed to do, Teddy. I'm so proud of you. You knew exactly what to do when the bill came."

"And guess what, Mimi; Christie even gave me refills."

Later, Mom told me not to sign any bills unless she or Dad was with me. I guess my tip was too much!

Besides hanging out at the pool, we went sightseeing during the days and to luaus at night. One time when we went to the Danny Couch show. I got to go up on stage and do the hula while Danny Couch sang. We went to that show almost every year, so I made sure I practiced the hula before we went. I was always thrilled when I was asked to do the hula on stage. Danny even gave me a grass skirt to wear!

One night Dad had a dream that he would find money on the ocean floor. So the day we went snorkeling, Dad combed through the sand with his hand, and sure enough, he started finding coins. Quarters, dimes, and pennies! Because he was so lucky, I started looking for buried treasure. But the only thing I found was a tire. It was pretty cool though. I called everyone over when I found it. Dad helped me pull it onto the shore. He wouldn't let me keep it though.

"It won't fit in our suitcase," he said.

Unfortunately, when Dad put on his snorkeling mask and dove back into the ocean, he couldn't find any more coins.

While we were in Hawaii, our family always had breakfast together at the Tapa Room. For two weeks, the waiters and waitresses there were our friends. Our waitress named Carol even asked us over to her condo for dinner. We met all her Hawaiian friends and ate Hawaiian ribs, octopus, poi, and coconuts. The last year we went, my parents gave Carol a Cincinnati basket containing Skyline Chili, Montgomery barbecue sauce, and Frische's tartar sauce.

Some days I would get really tired when we went sightseeing, because we had too many late nights and early breakfasts. On those days, my mom would take me back to the hotel room. Then my brother and cousins would all look at each other and say, "BEACH DAY!" That meant everyone would go to the pool and beach, instead of another tour. I would sleep in my room until about noon or later, and then I would feel better. I loved those vacations!

WHILE DAVID WAS AT BUTLER, I met lots of his friends and their families.

David's closest friends in college were, as my Mimi calls them, the "Butler Boys." My freshman year in high school they volunteered to help with my Special Olympic ski trip at Perfect North Slopes in Indiana. Mom and Dad couldn't go, but our class at Colerain needed volunteers, so I asked David. He said, "Let me see what I can do." He called all the guys and they took off work to come and help with the ski trip. They all had their own skis. They said they were weekend skiers, but they looked like professionals to me. As you can probably guess, skiing was not for me. David really tried to keep me up on the skis but it didn't work. After four or five tries down the bunny slope with the rope tow, he took me inside and bought me hot chocolate. I told him, "I quit. This is not my sport!" He went back out and helped all the other kids trying to ski. I told my mom and dad when I got home, "Do not buy me skis for Christmas or my birthday. I did not like that sport!" David told them that he and the other guys had never been so tired. They really got a workout helping me and my Special Olympic friends.

We still belong to the Touchdown Club, even though we don't get to many games. Coach LaRose is still at Butler as the Assistant Athletic Director. He always sends me birthday cards and Butler t-shirts. That's a good thing, because I still wear a lot of Butler gear. The "Butler Boys" send me cards too, and they come to many of my events and award presentations. They even came to my 30th birthday party. They are all married now and have children. Ben works for a medical firm that makes pacemakers. He was at the hospital when my Mimi had her pacemaker replaced two years ago. Toby works in Indianapolis as a vice-president at Remy, Inc., and Keoni is in charge of the Renaissance Hotel in Cincinnati. Kevin and David work at Aflac together.

NOW THAT YOU KNOW A LITTLE about my brother, you won't believe what happened when he was getting married. Not at the wedding, but the day before.

Everyone was so excited that my brother was getting married, because he was the first guy from the Butler Boys to do so. The wedding was on a Saturday and Tom, David's future father-in-law, arranged a golf outing on Friday for friends and family. I was invited to go along, too. When we got to the Pebble Creek Golf Course, my brother insisted I ride with him. His team played really well, and they even had several birdies. I was hoping someone would get a hole in one. By the time we got to the seventh hole, David's team was two under par. He was really excited as we pulled up to the green. I waited in the cart as David walked up the steps to finish out the hole.

When he finished, he asked me to drive the cart to the opposite side of the green.

"Pull up right behind the other cart," he said.

I thought he was kidding, so I asked him, "Me?"

"Yeah, you. You can do it. Just push on the pedal."

I remember thinking I can do this. Just push on the pedal like David said.

So I slid over behind the wheel and pushed on the pedal. I pushed harder than I should have, because the cart jumped forward and almost threw me out of my seat. I got scared and tugged on the steering wheel. The cart turned away from the path and started going up the steep hill that led to the green. The cart started leaning to the left, and my brother and his friends started yelling, "Teddy! Jump!" They all ran as fast as they could towards me.

But it was too late. The cart leaned to the left and then began to roll over. I tried to hang on to both sides of the seat, but I couldn't. I put my feet on the ground just as the open part of the cart rolled over me. For a second I was standing inside the cart, and then it turned over one more time and was upside down right beside me. David, Kevin, and my cousin Eddie grabbed the cart and stopped it from rolling again.

David shook his head and gave me a big hug. "I'm glad you're in one piece, Teddy."

"Are you kidding me," my cousin Eddie said. "How on Earth did that happen?"

I didn't know what to say.

We pushed the cart back onto its wheels. The top had a small dent in it and there were some scratches on the side.

Ben and Toby, who were in the group right behind us, yelled. "That was crazy!"

My brother gave them the okay sign, and then said to Eddie, "Let's move on. At least we parred the hole."

As we got into the cart, I asked David, "Want me to drive?" I was joking but he wasn't sure.

"No!"

We played the rest of the round and then headed back to Tom's house for a cookout. In the parking lot David said very firmly, "In no uncertain terms are you ever to tell Mom and Dad that you rolled over in the cart. At least, not until after the wedding. Mom and Dad don't need to hear how you almost killed yourself with the golf cart. Okay?"

I nodded and said, "Sure, I promise. I won't tell them."

When we arrived at Tom's house, Dad asked me how the day went. I smiled my widest grin, and said, "I rolled over in the golf cart!"

My brother's face turned red. He turned to me and said, "Can't you keep a secret for ten minutes?!"

"I couldn't help it," I told him. "It just sort of came out."

David ran his fingers through his hair and said, "I guess it did."

We told Mom about it on the Sunday after the wedding. She had too many other things on her mind.

DAVID AND ERIN'S WEDDING WAS A big event, especially for me. I remember when David told us he was getting married. He had been out of school for three years and was working at Aflac in Indianapolis. He called one Friday in September and said he was coming for dinner on the weekend. "Make sure you are home, Teddy. I have something special to tell you." David arrived Saturday night as Dad was grilling steaks. He took me aside and said, "Teddy, how would you like to be my best man at my wedding?"

"You're getting married?" I asked excitedly. "To Erin?"

"Of course, to Erin!" He paused. "So? Will you be my best man?"

I always knew I would be in David's wedding but to be his best man was huge!

"Yes! Yes!" I yelled as I ran up and hugged my brother.

David then said, "As the best man, you have to give a toast at the reception. You will also be in charge of the rings."

"Who's going to be the matron of honor?" I asked.

"Erin's asked her sister, Lee, to be the matron of honor. Erin's friend, Heidi, will be the maid of honor. They're going to give a toast, too. Oh yeah, and you'll have to get measured for a tux."

That was exciting. I had never worn a tuxedo before. I would look just like the announcers on Wide World of Wrestling.

The morning of the wedding the bridal party dressed in their rooms at the Marriott, a hotel across the river from Cincinnati. We had to get ready for pictures because the groomsmen were getting picked up around 10:30. The bridesmaids left much earlier because they were getting their hair done in Cincinnati. The entire wedding party was to meet in General James Taylor Park in Newport around 11. David wanted our pictures to be taken on the Kentucky side of the Ohio River so that the Great American Ball Park and Paul Brown Stadium would be in the background. The groomsmen and the bridesmaids were to meet in different parts of the park because David and Erin didn't want to see each other before the wedding. As the limo dropped us off in the park, I felt like I was in a spy movie! Teddy Kremer, alias James Bond! Kevin and Keoni looked around the area for any signs of the girls. Keoni heard giggling sounds near the playground and sure enough, he found the bridesmaid's location.

"Keep David away from the swings!" Keoni said.

The photographer took tons of pictures: the groomsmen and the bridesmaids together; David and the groomsmen; Erin and the bridesmaids; photos of just David; and photos of Erin by herself. Erin and David did not have their pictures taken together until after the wedding.

Right before we left for the wedding, David gave me Erin's wedding ring to put in my pocket for safekeeping. I checked on the ring every five minutes until we arrived at the church. While I was ushering Mimi down the aisle, I said to her, "I have Erin's wedding ring!" I was so excited.

"I know you will do a wonderful job, Teddy!" she said.

My other Mimi, my Mimi-Over- the-River, was in a wheelchair. As I pushed her down the aisle, I whispered to her about the ring. She smiled and winked at me.

As the ceremony started, I walked slowly down the aisle with Lee, just like Father Leo had taught us. In my mind I heard his words, "This is not a foot race, men and women. This is a wedding, one of God's greatest sacraments."

Once down the aisle, Lee turned left and stood next to the other bridesmaids. I turned right and stood right next to my brother throughout the ceremony. When it was time to exchange vows, Father Leo asked me for the rings. But when I put my hand down in my pocket, I couldn't find the ring. I saw David look over at my mom and dad and raise his eyebrows and smile as I dug deep into my pocket. The tuxedo pants had the deepest pockets. I struggled and finally I pulled the ring out! I had to reach almost down to my socks to find the ring. Those tuxedo pants were too long for my short legs.

At the reception I stood up and gave a toast. "Let's raise our glasses and toast my brother and new sister, Erin. Welcome to the family, Erin. I love you both! Cheers!"

Everyone said I did a great job. Both of my Mimis cried! I was relieved because I had been practicing every night for two whole weeks.

After the reception dinner, I danced with all our family and friends. I love to dance! The DJ was great and played some really good music. He had been warned by Erin not to give the microphone to anyone. She was afraid some of the younger people would get carried away and take over the microphone. Like me! I talked the DJ into giving me the microphone so I could perform a song by the Backstreet Boys. The DJ played "Everybody (Backstreet's Back)," and I got up on the stage and performed the whole song doing all the Backstreet Boys' dances and moves. Everybody cheered me on, so the DJ played the song again. Some of the guests in the back of the room stood on their chairs so they could see me better. I think I embarrassed my parents but everyone clapped when I got down from the stage. Some of David's friends asked if I would dance at their weddings. I know Kevin and Keoni really liked my moves. Even Erin was okay with it. I love having a sister like Erin.

The next day, good friends and family came over to our house for an early afternoon grill out. David and Erin spent the night, and then flew out the next morning for their honeymoon in the Mexican Riviera.

I KNOW MY BROTHER LOVES ME very much, and he has shown that in so many ways, even at his work. After David had been working at Aflac for a few months, he was invited to give a speech at the Indiana State Meeting, called "My Aflac Story." David's boss, John Tyler, suggested David give a speech about me. Erin was invited too, and she videotaped David on her phone so my parents and I could watch it later. For his speech, David talked about growing up in Cincinnati, his college days, and his experiences as an Aflac rep. Then he talked about me. David said his life had changed for the better after I was born. "Teddy has gone to therapy since he was two weeks old. He struggled all his life to reach new levels of learning. Things didn't come easy for Teddy, but he never gave up."

He then told everyone I was his hero and he was proud of me. "I have been very blessed to have a brother with Down syndrome. Because of Teddy, I understand the meaning of unconditional love, and I see my own challenges differently. Teddy has taught me that life is so much bigger than my own selfish setbacks and triumphs. Life is about accepting all people as human beings, no matter what their abilities or disabilities. Our family has always seen Teddy as a blessing, not a burden. I pray for a day that all parents with Down syndrome children embrace and love their children the way my parents love Teddy."

Erin said after David's speech there was not a dry eye in the house.

Recently, David invited my mom to go on an Aflac cruise to the Bahamas with him. Erin couldn't go because of her work schedule. She's a state government manager for Ikaso Consulting, and travels a lot for her job. Mom was thrilled and spent weeks packing and repacking. She called David constantly asking about what clothes to bring. After she left with David, Dad and I hung out and ate lots of pizza and Skyline chili. We had a great time baching it. The day before Mom came home, we spent all day cleaning up.

When Mom came home she couldn't wait to tell us all about the trip. She said at dinner one night a sales rep from Michigan asked David if he had any brothers or sisters. David said, "I have one brother who is younger than me."

The rep asked, "Who does he work for?"

David said, "I have a very special brother. He has Down syndrome and does a lot of inspirational talks. I may have him come and speak to our Aflac group one time." David continued, "In fact, Teddy was the batboy for the Cincinnati Reds."

Before David could say another word, the rep said, "He was

on *E:60*. I saw that piece! Wow! That's your brother? I loved that segment!"

David smiled. "Yes, I am very proud of my brother."

My mom said some of the people on the cruise remembered David's Aflac story from ten years ago, and they asked all about me.

Chapter 17

WHEN I WAS LITTLE WE WOULD VISIT MY GRANDPARENTS FOR Thanksgiving. I had two sets of grandparents. One year we would go to our Mimi and Papa's who live closest to us; the next year we would go to my Mimi and Papa's who live over the river. Both sets of grandparents always cooked big meals with turkey, dressing, sweet potatoes, and cranberry jelly. I couldn't bring myself to eat any turkey, not after what I learned in history class about the President pardoning a turkey every year. I ate my usual chicken nuggets with barbeque sauce and mashed potatoes.

When I was at Mimi-and-Papa-Over-the River's, we would see Aunt Sue, Uncle Greg, and my cousins Brian and Beth. When we had Thanksgiving at my other Mimi and Papa's, we would see my Uncle Ed, Aunt Caryl, and my cousins Alissa, Kristin, and Eddie. As I got older, Mom invited everybody to our house for Thanksgiving. She said it made things easier for the family. Then the family started growing, and people moved out of town, and not everyone could make it for Thanksgiving.

Now we go to David and Erin's house for Thanksgiving. Erin's whole family comes, too. We always have so much fun! The younger people play football while David smokes a turkey on his grill. It snows a lot in South Bend, but it never stops us from playing football. Even Dad and Tom play sometimes. Mom and Leslie stay in the house cooking away. They even make an oven-roasted turkey, in case the smoked turkey isn't enough. I have finally learned to like turkey, and David always saves a turkey leg for me.

The Friday or Saturday after Thanksgiving, we go to the Butler

Tree farm in Dowagiac just over the Indiana-Michigan state line to pick out David and Erin's tree. They have all kinds of animals and a little shop that has homemade cookies and the best hot chocolate! The lady in the cookie house always has special cookies for me. She told me Santa and the Butlers were wondering what day I would be there to see them. I love that place—it's magical.

When we get to the farm, we peek into Santa's little house to see if he is there. But David says we have to find a Christmas tree before we visit Santa. Luckily, David and Erin are really fast at finding the tree they like. Not like my parents. I thought when I was young we were going to be at the White House tree farm until after dark! After David and Erin find their perfect tree, we take a family picture. Then my nephews and I hike back up to Santa's house. I always go in to see Santa. He remembers my name and is glad to see me. Santa always says, "Ho! Ho! It's good to see you, Teddy. Have you been good this year?" The first year Trey was afraid of Santa, so I had to tell Santa what Trey wanted for Christmas. Now that he is a little older, Trey will talk to Santa, but Cord won't. Maybe he will sometime soon. I love it because it reminds me of when I was little, and I would go with Aunt Joan and Uncle Terry and their children, Ricky and Katie, to cut our tree down.

As much as I loved Thanksgivings growing up, I liked Christmases even more. We followed the same tradition every year. On Christmas Eve, we attended 3:00 PM Mass at St. Louis Church, and then we would go to my Over-The-River grandparents. We would have an early dinner and then open presents with my Aunt Sue and Uncle Greg and their children. On Christmas Day we would go to my other Mimi and Papa's house and have Christmas with my mom's side of the family. Later in the day, Mimi and Papa Over-the-River would come to our house for dinner. Once I started high school, we started going to Aunt Sue and Uncle Greg's house for Christmas Eve, and then everyone from both sides came to our house for Christmas Day.

EVEN THOUGH JANUARY IS GREAT BECAUSE it's my birthday month, it's really, really cold. I don't like to go outside in the cold, but at least I can continue swimming for the Special Olympic team, and practicing my ballroom dancing with Mary Cook at her dance studio.

People often ask me how I got involved in ballroom dancing. It was my Mimi who suggested it. She called my mom and told her about an article she read in the *Cincinnati Enquirer*.

At first my mom was reluctant to sign me up. "Really, Mom?" she said to Mimi. "Don't you think Teddy has enough going on? That's really a big commitment."

"But, Cheryl, you know how Teddy loves to dance. He's a natural. Plus, he'll be around people his own age."

"Mother, most of the people who take ballroom dancing are way older than Teddy."

"Well, you never know, dear. I read in *Senior Living* that a lot of younger people are taking it up."

"Whatever, Mom. I'll check it out."

So the first Wednesday of October in 2011, my mom took me to the A-Marika dance studio in Evendale, a half-hour ride from our home. My mom was really nervous about the dance class; you would have thought she was the one signing up for lessons! But there was nothing to worry about. My teacher, Mary Ramirez-Cook, and I liked each other right away. Mary told me she had been dancing since she was three years old and that she used to teach for Fred Astaire Studios and Arthur Murray before opening her own studio. Mary has five children, and her youngest child, Matthew, has Down syndrome, just like me. Maybe that's why we get along so well, or maybe that's why she is so good at teaching me all the hard steps. Mary started her class for young adults with Down syndrome because of Matthew. She thought it would be great exercise for us and increase our motor control. The class I attend is free.

Mary has what she calls volunteers who are her students in her other dance classes that come every Wednesday night to dance with all of us. They are excellent dancers and help us with our dance moves. It is a blast!

I continue to go there every Wednesday night and it is one of my favorite classes, because I not only get to dance with other people with Down syndrome around my same age, I also get to dance with the volunteers. We do all kinds of dances. Sometimes we do smooth dances, like the waltz and tango and fox-trot. Other times we practice Latin dances, like the rumba, salsa, and chi-chi; and sometimes Mary adds in some swing and country two step. My favorite dances are the fox-trot and the Viennese waltz.

I hate to miss Wednesday nights, because it's more fun to dance with lots of people. Besides the volunteers, I dance with some of the girls with Down syndrome. Sherry is a volunteer, and I have taught her the waltz the way Mary teaches me. I already knew some of the people there from the Special Olympics, but I have made two new dancing friends, Katie and Jill.

I take private lessons on Thursday nights, and it was during one of these lessons that Mary mentioned that the Butler County Board of Developmental Disabilities wanted Mary to dance at their Dancing for the Stars exhibition. Mary asked if I would be her dance partner for the event, and I immediately said, "Yes!" The night of our performance we danced to "The Starlight Waltz." I wore a formal tuxedo vest and a shiny silver tie. When we were finished, Mary and I received a standing ovation. That was the first time I danced in front of an audience, but it wouldn't be my last.

I guess I did so well at that Dancing for the Stars event, Mary invited me to be her dance partner in a dance competition. It would take place in the winter, and we would compete against dancers and their students. The dancers would come from all over the country. I was so excited about the competition, I told Mom before we left the dance studio.

"Are you sure you want to do this?" Mom asked on the way home.

"I would love to be in a dance contest. Maybe I can even get on the real *Dancing with the Stars*. I love that show; I've always wanted to dance with Cheryl Burke. My favorite dance ever on *Dancing with the Stars* was when Drew Lachey and Cheryl Burke danced the freestyle to "Save a Horse, Ride a Cowboy." That was so cool!

"Well, I guess Mimi was right all along. You do enjoy dancing and you are good at it," Mom sighed.

So, in the winter of 2012 I competed in the River Front Dance competition. Once inside the ballroom, I was really nervous, but I tried not to let it show. I kept telling Mom I was fine, but there was a huge crowd and half of them were professional dancers. Finally, Mary directed me to the center of the dance floor. First, we had thirty seconds to dance the waltz, fox-trot, and tango. We didn't know the music in advance, so we had to listen to each song, and dance accordingly. There were twenty couples on the floor with us, and they looked really good. But not good enough! Mary and I won first place in this segment of the competition. I was so excited!

Then Mary and I had to do our solo exhibition—the waltz. When we stepped out on the floor all eyes were on us. I said to myself, "You can do this, Teddy." Later Mary said to Mom and Dad, "I didn't think I could get Teddy to use the whole dance floor." But, I had no problem following her lead, and everyone gave us a standing ovation! I was in shock and then came another surprise—the judges asked us to return that evening and compete with two other couples for the winning trophy! We did, and we won second place! The judge said if we had a story to go with our routine, we might have won first place. Afterwards, Mary worked on putting a story to all of our dances.

Since then, I have competed in several contests. Most of the competitions are held in the convention center in Covington, Kentucky, which is just across the river from Cincinnati. In a 2013 competition, I danced the fox-trot to Todd Frazier's theme song, "Fly Me to the Moon." Mary was dressed as an umpire with a catcher's mask, and I was in my Reds uniform. While Mary and I were dancing, there was a problem with the sound equipment and our song stopped playing. Mary said, "Keep dancing our story and smile." Mary and I sang the song to each other as we danced, so our timing wouldn't be off. Then the next thing I knew, the entire audience was singing along to Todd's theme song. Some people pulled out their phones and found the song on their playlist and held up their phones so I could hear the music.

Mom had tears in her eyes because the audience did that for me. After we finished the dance, the judges remarked, "That was a great warm up, but we have the system fixed, and now you can give your real performance." So Mary and I danced again. We were so full of confidence, we didn't make one mistake. I ended up winning my competition in three categories, including the waltz and the cha-cha.

Mary was given a "Point of Light" award last year for the dance classes she has for young adults with Down syndrome. Mary doesn't charge any money for these classes, and all of our costumes for group performances come from donations. Right after she received the award, several reporters visited our Wednesday night dance class and took pictures for the Points of Light website. That was really cool, and our entire class is in one of the pictures.

Mary's classes and ballroom competitions are not the only places I dance. Sometimes I dance down the aisle as I go up to give a speech. Other times I dance for the students when I visit schools. I even danced at Colerain High for a fundraiser the school had. It was pretty cool to go back to my old school and dance with Mary in front of everyone. I wish I had danced like that when I was in school!

ANOTHER INTEREST OF MINE IS HORSEBACK riding. In 2004, my mom's friend Betsy Schulte told her about the Special Riders group at Winton Woods Park. My mom put me on the waiting list, and the next year we received the call that my name had made it to the top of the list. I kept telling Mom I was going to ride just like Chuck Norris in the television show *Walker, Texas Ranger*. But first I had to learn how to ride! One of my first horses was Tin Man. He was really nasty to everyone, but not to me. He would eat apples and carrots right out of my hand. He was a beautiful white Arabian, and boy was he big. I rode with the Special Riders for a while, but then I became more and more independent as a rider.

My trainer told my parents that she thought I was ready for the Special Olympics Equestrian Group for the state of Ohio. Because Tin Man was too old for the Special Olympics, my trainer assigned me a new horse.

His name is Chevy and he's mostly brown. In the middle of his forehead is a white mark that looks just like the symbol on a Chevrolet truck. Chevy was great, except he kicked the other horses when they came too close to me. Initially, Chevy would tense up when I rode him. He probably sensed my uneasiness, because I never knew when he was going to start kicking. Every time he kicked, I felt like I was going to fall off and land on my head. My trainer told me to lean forward and rub his neck. She also encouraged me to talk to him in a soft voice. Eventually, we became really good friends and now we love each other.

I entered many competitions with Chevy, such as trail riding and barrel racing. Sometimes during the events Chevy would get all worked up and run out from under me. There have been many times when I thought I was going to fall off that horse, but I learned to lean way over and grab the saddle horn so I could pull myself back up.

I also compete in Western Working Equitation. In this event, I'm the one being judged, not my horse. It's all about how I sit on the horse and hold my posture. I am also judged on how I handle my horse. The judges will ask me to have Chevy walk, reverse, trot, and then walk again. Since I ride Western style, my boots must be polished before and after I mount. I wear a western shirt and a bolo tie. I try to keep calm when I ride past the judges, but inside I am all nervous and jumpy. Some of the ribbons I have won are on my bedroom wall at home. Dad told me one time, "I never thought I would see you win at barrel racing."

"Me either, but it sure was fun winning!" I said. "When can I get my own horse?"

"Someday, maybe," Mom said.

I frowned, because I have heard enough "somedays" to know that I'm not getting a horse.

I still swim for the Ohio Special Olympics, but not like I used to. Between Fifth Third Bank, the Reds, dancing, horseback riding, giving speeches, and going to La Rosa's, I don't have a lot of spare time. I barely have enough time to watch my Disney shows anymore!

Chapter 18

A FEW YEARS AGO, SOMETHING HAPPENED THAT CHANGED MY life forever. It's probably the reason you have heard of me.

Every year Mom and Dad go to a fundraiser given by Mercy Montessori, where I went to preschool, elementary, and junior high. The auction is Mercy's biggest fund raising event, and the proceeds from the event provide scholarships for low-income families. On that special night in March of 2012, Dad saw something on the silent auction table that caught his eye. "Cheryl, did you see this?" he asked Mom.

She looked and there was a certificate to be batboy for the Cincinnati Reds. It was for only one game, but it was my Cincinnati Reds. My favorite team ever! How cool is that? At first my parents were excited, but then they read the fine print: *Winner must be between 13 and 19 years old.*

"Well, maybe they will make an exception for Teddy," Dad said.

Mom said they continued to look at the auction items and talk to their friends, but then they spotted Phil Castellini. He's the Reds Chief Operating Officer, and his children go to Mercy.

Dad went over to him and introduced himself. "My son is a huge fan of the Reds," Dad said.

"Well," Mr. Castellini said, "you should bid on the chance for him to be batboy for a day."

Mom said, "We are thinking about bidding, but our son is twenty-nine years old, and has Down syndrome, but he acts like he's fifteen."

Mr. Castellini didn't hesitate. "If you win, we'll make it happen."

Mom then said, "You know, Teddy graduated from Mercy, and he loves the Reds."

Patty Normile, the principal of Mercy (and my former teacher), walked over just then. "You will love Teddy, and he'd make a great batboy," she told Mr. Castellini.

Mr. Castellini thought for a moment and then smiled at my parents. "Like I said, If you win the bid, we'll make it work. I look forward to meeting Teddy someday."

My parents told me that they started the bid at $300, and strangely enough no one at the event bid against them. In later years, the winning bid for batboy has gone for over $3,000.

My parents didn't tell me about winning the bid for batboy until late July, because they didn't want me to be disappointed if it didn't all work out. I found out later that MLB has a rule that an honorary batboy must be 13- to 19-years-old with no "limitations." I think that means no special needs people like me. So, Phil Castellini went to his dad, Bob, the owner of the Reds, and said that he made a promise to the Kremers and wanted to keep it. So Bob Castellini called the Commissioner of MLB and explained the situation. The Commissioner finally, in July, gave the Reds permission to have me as their honorary batboy. Later the Commissioner told the Castellinis that having me as the batboy was great for baseball.

In late July my parents received a phone call from Diana Busam, the executive assistant to Phil Castellini. She wanted to set up a time for me to come to the ballpark and do a tour.

That night at dinner Dad sat me down at the kitchen table. "Teddy," he said, "we have something to tell you."

"Is something wrong?" I asked.

"No, just the opposite," Dad said. "Remember when we went to Mercy's Spring Fling last March? Well, while we were there we bid on a chance for you to be batboy for a day."

"Batboy? For whom?"

"The Cincinnati Reds."

"What?!"

"We won the bid and you're going to be the Reds batboy for a day."

When Dad's words sunk in, I jumped out of my chair, raised my fists, and yelled, "Yes!" I could not have been more excited if I had won a trip to the moon. The Cincinnati Reds! I ran around the house with my hands in the air and couldn't stop smiling. Mom said later she thought I would never calm down. But I finally calmed down enough to start asking questions.

"When? What do I do?"

"The game isn't for a while and we don't really know what your responsibilities will be, but it will be a good chance for you to meet some of the players," Dad said.

That was exciting enough, but I still made up my mind to be the best batboy ever.

THE FIRST WEEK OF AUGUST, THE Reds invited my parents and me down to a game. I guess they wanted to check me out to make sure I could do the job as batboy. So that afternoon, Diana Busam met us at Gapper's Alley, the entrance into the ballpark for special guests. From there she took us to the broadcast booth and to the media center where all the sports writers watch the game and write their stories about the Reds. When we were in the broadcast booth, I spoke to Marty Brennaman, the radio announcer for the Reds. I blurted out, "You look good without your hair." Mom rolled her eyes at that one.

Marty remembered me from when he spoke at the Colerain Stag. He said, "I've met this young man before. Teddy, right?"

I nodded and said, "I really like your hair since you shaved it." Marty had made a bet earlier in the season that if the Reds won ten games in a row, he would shave his head for donations to the

Dragonfly Foundation, a group that helps children and young adults with cancer.

"Thanks," Marty said. "Yours looks good, too."

"Next," Diana said, "we're going to the Reds clubhouse. Follow me, we have to go down several ramps to get there."

We ended up at the clubhouse entrance of my Cincinnati Reds! Once we were in the clubhouse office, Diana instructed us to put our cell phones and cameras away. "Sorry, we can't disturb the Reds with pictures or autographs. They have a job to do, you know."

"That's okay, I didn't bring my phone or camera with me. I promise I won't bother the players."

After a few minutes, Phil Castellini came into the office and greeted us. "Teddy, wait here a minute. I have someone really important I want you to meet."

Then Phil went into the locker room to find Rick Stowe, the home clubhouse and equipment manager. Mr. Stowe was really excited to meet us, and then the unthinkable happened. Mr. Stowe took *me* back into the Reds clubhouse. Can you believe it? I was going into the locker room where all of my favorite players were! It was almost too much! But it was really cool. I met Rick Stowe's son Luke, who was the regular batboy. He told me, "Don't worry about anything when you are out there, Teddy. I will be with you the whole time."

Then I walked around and met some of the players. When I first saw Zach Cosart, I walked up to him and said, "Zach, so good to meet you!" Then I gave him a high five. Before I could introduce myself to the other players, Chris Heisey came up to me and said, "Teddy, we're so glad you are going to be with us." Even Dusty Baker came over and said, "We are glad to have you here." Though Diana told me not to bother anyone, I still gave Dusty a hug. I couldn't help myself!

When Rick Stowe brought me back to the office, he gave Mr. Castellini the thumbs up and said, "Teddy is ready to go! We will have a jersey for him on game night." He also told me the Reds would give me my own jersey to keep, and I could choose my own number. I picked 32, Jay Bruce's number, because when we were in the 2010 playoffs against the Houston Astros, Jay Bruce, with two strikes and two balls, hit a walk off home run to make the Reds the National League champs.

Then Mr. Bob Castellini walked into the office. I stood up and said, "Mr. Castellini, it so nice to meet you. You have a great team!"

He shook my hand and said, "You must be Teddy! I hear you are going to be batboy for us on August 17."

I smiled and said, "I'm so excited. I promise I will do a great job as batboy."

"I'm sure you'll do a wonderful job, Teddy. Have you enjoyed yourself today?"

"Yes, sir, I sure have. And now I get to watch the Reds play!"

We watched the game in Scout's Alley, right behind the diamond seats. Bronson Arroyo pitched a great game and the Reds won. The whole day was so exciting. I couldn't wait until August 17, the day I would be the honorary batboy!

I told everyone I knew that I was going to be the batboy for the Reds. Most of our friends and family bought tickets to the game.

ERIN, TREY, AND CORD CAME TO Cincinnati the night before my big game, and stayed with us. My brother brought a group of his Aflac co-workers down to the game for winning a sales contest, but they stayed downtown at the Westin.

I was so excited the night before the game that I could barely sleep. To think that I would be down on the field, in the dugout, in front of thousands of people was more than I could stand. I couldn't wait to see the players and coaches again. Just think, Joey Votto, Brandon Phillips, Todd Frazier, and the rest of the team would depend on me to take care of their bats!

The morning of August 17, Mom fixed all of us pancakes and bacon. As I ate my breakfast, she reminded me, "You know this will go by fast, so make sure you enjoy every second." Well, I knew that would be easy to do because I loved the Cincinnati Reds. They were, and still are, my favorite team. I get really excited when we win, and I usually cry when we lose. I can't help it. I have Reds hats and banners, autographed baseballs, bobble heads, and lots of Reds baseball cards all over my bedroom. I even have pictures of Ken Griffey, Jr., Jay Bruce, and Cincinnati's hit king, Pete Rose, hanging on my walls.

Way before I became batboy for the Reds, Mom, Dad, and I always watched the Reds on television and attended at least three or four games during the season. Usually, we sat along the first or third baseline, so I could catch foul balls. One time, Todd Frazier hit one that looked like it was coming right at us. It landed a few rows behind us and bounced off one of the seats and came towards me. I wasn't fast enough to catch the ball, but the guy next to me had his glove out and the ball went right in it. After that night, I made sure I always I had my glove ready.

The day seemed to drag on and on, and I kept asking Mom and Dad questions. "What time are we going to leave to meet David? I won't be late, will I? Do you think the Reds will like me?"

Mom tried to calm me down, telling me that we would be on time and that I would do a great job. "But if the Reds don't win, you still have to be a good sport."

"Oh, no," I told her, "The Reds will win by a lot." Mom said she hoped so for my sake. "Mom, you know we can't let the Cardinals catch us," I said. "They always win the pennant. This year it's our turn."

MOM SAID I HAD TO BE ready by 2:30, so an hour before we left, I put on my khaki shorts, my Reds t-shirt, and my black gym shoes.

The day before, Dad bought me new black gym shoes, because Rick Stowe said that's what the Reds wanted me to wear. I wore the shoes around the house to break them in, but I always kept them in the box when I wasn't wearing them. That way they would be shiny for the game. To finish my outfit, I put on one of my Reds baseball hats and looked at myself in the mirror. And just like every guy who ever dreamed about becoming a big league player, I pretended I was up to bat with the bases loaded and a full count. *Here's the pitch to Big Teddy,* I imagined. *It's a long drive to center field…it's gone!*

After I was satisfied with my baseball look, I ran up the stairs and told Mom and Dad I was ready.

"I think you're batting cleanup tonight," Dad said.

"No, I'm just the batboy," I answered.

"Well, you never know," he said with a smile.

Mom took some pictures of me and we piled into the car. On the way down, Dad said, "You know, they might let you on the field for a minute or two to meet some players but once the game starts, you'll probably have to sit with us."

I hoped that wasn't the case, but I guessed Dad was right. "Just being on the field a little bit will be cool enough," I told him.

When we got close to downtown and the Ohio River, I could see the stadium ahead. We had been to lots of games before, but it felt different this time. It was too much to think about, so I promised to do like Mom said and enjoy every minute of the game.

We parked under the stadium and walked to the Holy Grail where David and his friends were waiting for us. Most of David's co-workers were from Granger, Indiana, and were Cubs fans. And guess who the Reds were playing that day—the Chicago Cubs! That's probably why David arranged the trip for them. Even though I had my Reds hat on, David's friends were really nice to me and wished me, "Good luck!"

After a snack at the Holy Grail, we made our way to Gapper's Alley. It was a long walk because we had to cross Joe Nuxall Way and walk up a long ramp. We met Diana Busam there, and she reminded me all about what I could do, what I should do, and what I couldn't do.

"I know," I said. "My mom and dad went over the rules with me already."

Then she walked us down the ramp and tunnel that leads to the clubhouse entrance. That is where I said goodbye to my parents.

Before Mom and Dad left, Mom told me not to bother the players. She said, "This is their job, so don't talk to them. And don't touch them."

I answered, "Don't touch them? Gee, Mom."

She patted my arm, "Well, I know how you get." Before my parents left, Mom and Dad gave me a hug. Dad said, "We are so proud of you, Teddy." I think he had tears in his eyes.

"Thanks for doing this for me," I said as I hugged Mom and Dad.

I saw Mr. Bob Castellini and shook his hand again. I was in the outer office of the Reds clubhouse. The man at the desk called back to the clubhouse and Rick Stowe came out to get me. He had my Reds uniform all ready for me. It was just like the players, except my uniform shirt said BB on the back, for batboy.

The first Reds player I saw was the manager, Dusty Baker. He was writing out the game's lineup card. He saw me with Mr. Stowe and said, "Thanks for helping out tonight." I really don't remember what I said, but I think it was, "This is so exciting!" He smiled and looked around the clubhouse, "Yes, it is. I have been around baseball for many years. I still love baseball and the excitement of the game."

He held the lineup card out for me to see. "This is who's playing tonight," he said.

"Oh, I know all about that," I told him. "You give it to the umpire before the game, so the other team can see who is about to beat them."

Dusty laughed at that. "They might be thinking that, but they give me a lineup card too, you know." Dusty then said he needed to go. "Watch out during batting practice. There'll be lots of balls flying around here. Keep your helmet on." I told him I would be careful, and then Mr. Stowe took me to meet Luke again, the regular batboy.

"Don't run out onto the field while the game is still going on," Luke said. *Like I would do that.* "And make sure you put the bat back in the right slot." All of a sudden I realized that I might actually be the batboy and not have to go sit with Mom and Dad. I think my eyes got wide because Luke asked me, "You getting this?"

He showed me where the players' bats go at the end of the bench in the dugout. Each player has a special place for his bat, so I had to be sure to put the bats in the correct places. I didn't want Zach Cozart reaching for his bat and, instead, picking up Brandon Phillips's bat. That would be a disaster for the Reds.

Soon the stadium was filling up with Reds and Cubs fans. The feeling I had looking up into the stands was hard to describe.

"It's pretty amazing seeing all the fans from down here, isn't it, Teddy?"

Luke was very patient with me, and told me again, "I will be right here to help you." Luke grew up around the Reds clubhouse, because his grandfather Bernie Stowe had been working for the Reds since the 1940s. He started out as a batboy, and eventually became the Reds director of equipment and clubhouse. He didn't retire until 2014. He once humorously told Sparky Anderson, former Reds manager, "Let's get one thing straight, I was here before you got here, and I'll be here after you're gone, so don't give me any crap." Bernie's son and Luke's dad, Rick, is now the Reds clubhouse manager.

Luke told me he knew exactly how I felt when I saw some of my favorite players close up, because he felt the same way, and he was around them every day. When he said that, I felt like I had butterflies in my stomach. Before I could get too overwhelmed, Luke showed me where to stand during the game. He took me out to the on-deck circle and explained how I should take the weighted bats and rosin bag out there when the Reds were batting. Then when the Reds made the third out, I would have to go and bring all the bats and bags back into the Reds dugout. It sure was a lot of putting and taking!

Right before the game, some of the players came out of the tunnel from the clubhouse to the dugout. Brandon Phillips and Joey Votto smiled at me and gave me thumbs up. Chris Heisey gave me a high-five, and Drew Stubbs shook my hand.

They could tell I was a little bit thrilled.

Brandon said, "I hope you have fun tonight. And make sure you rub some good luck on my bat."

Soon the players stepped onto the field to do their warm-ups and stretching. My parents and Erin and Trey had seats right behind the dugout. They didn't bother me because they knew I was busy with my job. Mostly I sat on the bench or stood on the steps of the dugout. Mom couldn't see me from her seat, and she told me later it drove her crazy wondering whether or not I was bothering the players. Since Sue and Tim Roedersheimer were sitting down the third baseline, they could see me just fine. They texted Dad and said I was all over the dugout high-fiving and talking to the players. Dad didn't tell Mom until later what they were texting. He said everything was okay, and I was being really cool about everything.

Todd Frazier came over and talked to me for a few minutes. I told him where I lived and that I was a huge fan of his. Todd is the third baseman for the Reds, and at that time he had only been on the team for a few years. He gave me a wristband to wear and so did Chris Heisey. Chris spent some time talking to me about all kinds of things, like my favorite sports and what sports I played. Chris acted like I was a friend and it was normal for me to be in the dugout. Then he grabbed his glove off the bench as a couple of other players gave me a pat on the back. "Have fun tonight," someone said.

While the outfielders were tossing the balls around, the umpires gathered at home plate with the Cubs manager. I've always wondered what they talked about out there. Before I had time to think too much about it, Dusty waved to me from the on-deck circle. "Come with me, Teddy."

I went up the steps onto the field and then turned to Luke and mouthed, "Is this okay?" Luke smiled and shook his head, "Yes!" So I walked with Dusty to home plate where the Cubs manager, the umpires, and the Reds honorary captain were talking. Dusty handed me the lineup card on our way to the plate. "Now you give this to the umpire, Teddy," Dusty said.

"Me?" I asked.

Dusty smiled his famous smile and said, "Yes, you, Teddy!" Dusty introduced me to the umpires and we all shook hands. I gave the home plate umpire the Reds lineup card, and he explained the ground rules of the Great American Ballpark to the managers.

When I got back to the dugout, Hannigan, the catcher, was putting on his gear. The rest of the players were picking up their gloves and firing one another up because the game was about to start. Before I knew it, the announcer was saying, "Welcome to the Great American Ballpark for tonight's game between the visiting Chicago Cubs and your own Cincinnati Reds." Everybody in the stands cheered. Then the announcer said, "And a special welcome to tonight's honorary batboy, Teddy Kremer." I looked up and saw that I was on the big screen with Dusty. I didn't know they were going to do that! But I think Dusty knew that if I was with him, I would appear on the big screen. I couldn't help but look for Mom and Dad in the stands, but there were so many people wearing red and standing up that it was hard to find them.

The announcer told the fans to stand and remove their hats for the National Anthem. The players and I lined up in front of the dugout. I knew Chris Heisey always stood next to Dusty Baker during the National Anthem, so I was surprised when Dusty and

Chris had me stand between them. I had my left hand over my heart and I swear I could feel it beating. Chris Heisey whispered to me, "Other hand." I knew I was really nervous because I have always put the correct hand over my heart. I've done this since I was three years old at Mercy Montessori. I stood very straight as the players and crowd sang "The Star Spangled Banner." It was then that I realized I was going to be in the dugout the entire game! All of a sudden, I knew how important this night would be to me.

After the National Anthem, Luke called me over and handed me a bunch of baseballs. "You take these to the umpire."

I think my mouth fell open but I managed to say, "Me?"

"Yes, you," he said. So I walked up to home plate trying not to drop any of the balls. Mom said she almost fainted when she saw me walk out onto the field. She told Dad, "Oh, my, there's Teddy. What's he doing out on the field?"

Not knowing how nervous Mom was, I carefully handed the balls to the home plate umpire who immediately shoved them in his coat pocket.

"And now," the announcer said, "your Cincinnati Reds!" The announcer called out each player's name as they ran out of the dugout.

Bronson Arroyo was the Reds pitcher that evening, so I knew we had a really good chance of winning the game. After he got the Cubs out in the first inning, I gave him a high-five as he came into the dugout. Bronson was very talkative; he asked me if I played any sports.

"I'm on a softball team," I told him, "and I play second base just like Brandon. I like to dance and sing, too."

He thought that was cool and told Brandon Phillips, "You better watch out for Teddy!"

I felt so proud to be talking with him about something that I can do. For someone on the Reds to know that I love to dance and sing and play softball made me feel good. I then said, "If you ever want to play your guitar and sing while I dance, that would be fun."

"How do you know that about me?" Bronson asked with a big smile.

"I love the Reds and I know all about you guys. I know your batting averages and ERAs. Lots of stuff."

He laughed and so did a couple of players who heard me.

Then I told him, "When you won 17 games in 2010, it was great. I'm rooting for you to do it again."

He high-fived me and said, "Me, too, Teddy."

"I believe in you," I told him.

I collected all the weighted bats and rosin bags and took them to the on-deck circle. I had to be careful going to get the bats next to home plate. If a player got a hit, I had to wait till the umpire nodded for me to run up there. One time I almost ran out too soon and Luke put his hand on my arm. If the Reds got a hit and there was a player on base, I had to be sure I did not interfere with the play at home or somewhere on the field.

Dusty stood next to me a few times. He was quiet and chewed on a toothpick most of the game. But he did ask me a couple times what I thought. "We're okay, Dusty," I told him. "We're gonna win." He smiled and continued to chew on his toothpick.

In the second inning, the Cubs got a run but we tied it up in the bottom of the inning. They got a couple of runs in the fourth. When Bronson made it back to the dugout, I told him, "That's okay. We'll get some runs for you. You just wait."

In the bottom of the fourth, our first batter up was Ryan Ludwick. I was standing beside Dusty Baker when—on the very first pitch— Ryan hit it a mile into the left field seats. I ran out to get the bat and the crowd was going crazy. The next batter was Jay Bruce, and the pitcher hit him with the ball. It looked like it really hurt, but he just tossed his bat over toward me and ran to first. Up next was Todd Frazier, my favorite player. He swung and missed a couple of pitches. Then he hit one as far as the one Ryan hit! We were ahead! I ran out to home plate with my fists pumping in the air. When I got back to the dugout, Bronson said to me, "I guess you were right, Teddy." He smiled really big and both of us high-fived Todd.

"I knew we'd come back!" We never lost the lead after that.

As I was going to the plate to get Drew Stubbs's bat, Brandon Phillips was on his way to bat. I gave him a fist bump and he turned and smiled at me with his big happy smile. I didn't even know that it had happened until my mom, dad, and Erin told me about it. My mom said, "I told you not to touch them!" What she didn't know was that I was giving the players hugs and high-fives. The players acted like I was part of the team.

One inning I told Luke I had to go to the bathroom really, really bad. He said, "Run to the clubhouse while the Cubs are batting." When I got there, the only player down in the clubhouse was Johnny Cueto. Well, Johnny Cueto doesn't speak English, so I was hoping he understood me. When I asked, he pointed down a hallway. I ran to the restroom and still made it back to the dugout before the Cubs were out.

While the Reds were at bat, I stood on the dugout steps and folded my arms like the coaches. That's what coaches do when they are really serious. I talked a lot to Chris Steier. He was the bench coach for the Reds. I watched the game very carefully so I would know when I needed to go and pick up the bats. He helped me a lot and would stop me if I were going out too soon. Also, I paid close attention to the home plate umpire who would signal to Luke and me the amount of balls he needed. It was really hard carrying several baseballs at one time while running. I could see myself dropping the balls and then having to run around picking them up. Luckily, that didn't happen.

Like Mom had said it would, the game went by fast and before I knew it, our reliever Chapman finished the game. I could actually hear the ball hiss through the air as Chapman pitched.

In the bottom of the ninth inning, I was sitting on the bench next to Joey Votto. When Chapman got the second man out, I started to cheer, saying, "We won!"

Joey said to me, "Never cheer until the final out." I will always remember what Votto said.

We won 7-3. It was such a wonderful day. Todd Frazier asked me, "Did you have fun today?"

I really didn't have to answer since I was smiling as much as I could, but I said, "This is the greatest thing ever!" I love all the Reds, but Todd is one my favorites. I can't stand it when he doesn't get a hit or strikes out. I know he tries to do his best every time.

After the game Dusty told me to come out on the field to shake hands with the players like they do after every game the Reds win. After shaking hands with the players, I went into the clubhouse and gave Dusty a huge hug. "Thank you again!" I said. I told the players goodbye and gave them high-fives and hugged them, too. Behind me, one of the players yelled, "Great job, Teddy!" I turned around and gave a high-five to Todd Frazier. I was smiling ear to ear! I changed back into my street clothes, but I wore my uniform shirt the Reds gave me with Jay Bruce's number and my name on the back.

It was Fireworks Friday so the crowd stayed to watch the fireworks. Luke walked me through the Diamond Club to take me to where my parents, Erin, and Trey were sitting. Some of the fans in the Diamond Club stopped me and asked for pictures. With me? I was really surprised.

I finally got to Mom and Dad's seats. Trey was really excited to see me and wanted to know all about the game. We watched the fireworks together. People kept coming up to me and asking to shake my hand. My dad even said, "I didn't know that many people watch the batboy!" Even as we walked back to the car, the fans recognized me and called out, "Good job out there, Buddy!"

The next morning, there was a picture in the *Cincinnati Enquirer* showing me running back to the dugout with a bat. In the picture Brandon Phillips is standing behind me. I had just high-fived Brandon on the way back to the dugout and he's smiling at me.

Jeff Swinger, who went to D.C. with us, took the photo. Everyone seemed to like the picture. I have a copy of it on the wall in my room.

Soon after, John Erardi came to our house to interview me. He was really nice, and I felt like I had known him forever. I showed him the lineup card Dusty Baker autographed for me: "Teddy Kremer—The Good Luck Charm, Reds Win 7-3." John spent a long time at our house. I was more excited about making a new friend than his article.

A few weeks later our phone started ringing off the wall. My Aunt Sue, Lauren, Sean, and everyone was asking if we had seen the paper. It was my job to get the paper from the end of the driveway, but I had been busy watching *Sports Center* and hadn't gotten around to it yet. After so many calls, Dad ran out and got the paper, and there I was on the front page of the *Cincinnati Enquirer*.

John had written a long article about me. The headline read: "Ted Joined the Reds for the Day but Changed the Team Forever." I was so happy I helped my favorite team! When my mom called to thank him, he said the article was getting lots of attention and people as far away as South America, Australia, Malaysia, and Europe were tweeting him about how inspiring his article was. John wrote about what it meant to the players for me to be batboy. Brandon Phillips said, "Teddy showed us how to enjoy life, be yourself, go out and play hard." I never knew being a fan of a team was so important. I think everyone should feel the way I do, but I guess they don't.

People called me all day long when the article came out. I didn't know what to say, so I would just tell them, "I had fun and the players were great to me."

Chapter 19

ONE DAY IN LATE OCTOBER THERE WAS A MESSAGE ON OUR HOME answering machine from Megan Anderson at ESPN. She said she was a producer on ESPN's *E:60* and would like to talk to me about doing a feature story. Mom called her back, and Megan said she had family in Cincinnati and they had sent her John's article. Mom asked if by chance she was related to Ken Anderson, the former Cincinnati Bengals quarterback. It turns out Kenny Anderson is her father. He was the one who sent her the article! Before the conversation ended, Megan said she would be in touch with us again as soon as baseball season began.

I didn't think too much about that phone call, and just went on with my life, working, swimming, dancing, and riding. Then in February I went to the Colerain Stag, and believe it or not, the featured speaker was none other than Kenny Anderson. I had my picture taken with him and spent some time talking to him. The next week Megan called and said she had talked to her dad about me. She said he was really pumped about the possibility of a feature ESPN story about me and encouraged Megan to contact the Reds. Right after that phone call, ESPN started talking to Major League Baseball and the Reds. Megan told us that the Reds had to receive permission from MLB to have me back as batboy and to allow ESPN to film the game. February was an awesome month for me. Not only did I get a call from ESPN, that was the month I went to Washington, D.C., for the State of the Union Address.

That spring the *Cincinnati Enquirer* invited John Erardi and me to ride on their float for the Opening Day Parade. Opening Day in Cincinnati is a big deal; the Reds always open the season with a home game. I guess that's because the Cincinnati Red Stockings was the first professional team in the United States. The entire city practically closes down for the day so people can attend the parade. Students are even given permission to miss school for the game and the parade.

In 2013, Opening Day was on the Monday after Easter, April 1, and Megan called and told us ESPN would be filming me that day. They came to my house before the came and filmed me getting ready. That was really cool, especially since David, Erin, and the boys were there to watch. (They were still in town because of the Easter holiday). It was really cold outside, so I had to wear my long underwear and heavy coat. The *Cincinnati Enquirer* called right before we left and invited Dad to ride in the float with John and me; the three of us sat on the trunk of the *Cincinnati Enquirer's* convertible. A film crew from ESPN and Megan walked right next to our float, filming and recording everything we said. Someone from the crowd yelled, "We love you, Colerain!" Others yelled, "We love you, Teddy!" When we passed by Fountain Square, I saw Mom, David, Erin and the boys; they looked frozen.

The Reds also invited me to walk the red carpet on Opening Night, Wednesday, April 3. Opening Night in Cincinnati is another huge deal, and it always takes place on the first night game of the season. The radio and television announcers all wear tuxedoes, and the people that work at the Great American Ballpark wear tuxedo shirts.

The players walk on a red carpet in the Kroger fan zone, right outside the seating area, but still within the ballpark. An announcer introduces the players as they walk down the fancy carpet lined with fans, and the players sign autographs and have pictures taken with the fans. I walked down the carpet with Dusty Baker. It was fun signing autographs and talking to everyone. One fan took a picture of me, and said, "I work with your cousin Kristen. I'll send her your picture!"

My most important job of the night was to escort Miss Teen Ohio and Miss Ohio USA to the pitcher's mound with the game ball and rosin bag. After I dropped the girls off, I sneaked down to the dugout to see the players. Most of the players gave me hugs and high-fives, but I had to hurry away because the game was about to start. As I ran to the other side of the field to leave through the visiting team's dugout, the umpire waved at me and said, "Hey, Teddy, glad you're back!"

My parents told me that Phil Castellini spoke to them while I was walking down the red carpet. "So I hear Teddy's story is going national," he said. My parents laughed and said, "So we hear!"

A few days later, Megan called my dad and asked if I would like to be batboy for a second time on Thursday, April 18. She said ESPN and the Cincinnati Reds had made arrangements for me to be filmed that night. While I felt like a movie star, I did feel stressed because I usually work on Thursdays. Dad said not to worry about that; he felt certain Fifth Third Bank would give me the day off. But I wasn't so sure; things were happening way too fast. The good thing was that I already knew how to put the bats back and take balls to the umpire, so I didn't have to learn as much. Dad didn't have to convince me too much; I pretty much said yes right away.

For my birthday that year, my Uncle Ed and Aunt Caryl's family gave my parents and me tickets to the Reds game on Sunday, April 7. As we walked into the stadium, many people asked if they could have their pictures taken with me. I was really surprised because I wasn't in uniform. My dad and I went down to the dugout to wave at Todd, Dusty, and Luke Stowe right before we went to our seats. Johnny Cuerto was pitching, so I was really excited.

Our seats were in the top rows of the infield box section right behind home plate, so the sun was shining in our faces. My mom had forgotten the sunscreen, but the man sitting in front of us shared his sun block with us. I sat very still so no one would recognize me; I really wanted to focus on the game. Then in the middle of the game, Mr. Bob Castellini, the owner of the Reds walked past us and sat in the empty seat next to my mom. He came to see the gentleman with the sun block.

As it turns out, the two of them were old high school friends. I started to talk to Mr. Castellini, but Mom gave me the "don't say anything" look and put her finger to her lip. Mr. Castellini talked to his friend for a long time, and then started back across our row, apologizing to us. I was the last one in our row and when he saw me, he said, "Teddy, you're my batboy! What are you doing up here?" We laughed, and Mom and Dad moved over a seat so he could talk to me. After about ten minutes, he left to go back up to his box. "I'll see you in a couple of weeks!" I yelled after him.

IN THE DAYS LEADING UP TO April 18, my parents reminded me over and over again what Diana Busman had said: "The players have a job to do. There should not be any autographs or pictures. You can talk to the players when they want to talk."

My mom added, "Don't talk to the players or touch them." We both knew that usually doesn't work.

The night of April 18, the Reds expected me to get to the stadium early, just like last time. The Reds were playing the Miami Marlins; I think their nickname is "The Fish," which is pretty funny. ESPN came to our house in the afternoon and filmed me dressing, getting into the car, and riding down to the ballpark.

When we arrived at the Great American Ballpark, we went straight to Gapper's Alley. It was really hard to miss us coming. We had Rick the cameraman and Joe the sound tech, and another man carrying the boom mike. The boom mike is what *E:60* uses to record all the talking. They used it at the opening parade, too. People were staring at us, wondering what was going on. I just smiled and said, "Hello, how are you doing?"

Diana met us at the gate like she did last time. We walked down the ramp into the tunnels under the stadium to get to the players' locker room entrance. This was becoming a familiar walk for the four of us. At the clubhouse entrance I said goodbye to my parents, and Dad said, "Have fun and do a good job." Mom, of course, said, "Be good and remember…"

"I know, I know," I said laughing.

Luke was there to meet me. I really like Luke. He is in college and is really cool. He always treats me like a friend. He said he was there to help me, but knew I could handle the job. He had my uniform ready and this time he gave me a Reds Nike shirt to wear under my uniform instead of the regular white t-shirt I had worn last August.

In the locker room, I stopped by Dusty's office. He welcomed me again and said he would meet me in the dugout in a few minutes. I went to the main part of the locker room where the players were getting ready. I talked to everyone there: Todd Frazier, Jay Bruce, Brandon Phillips, and Joey Votto. Todd gave me a big high-five and so did Chris Heisey. Todd asked me about school, and I told him I graduated from Colerain High in 2004, and that we won the state championship for football when I was coach. He told me his parents were both teachers, which I thought was pretty cool, since both of my parents used to teach.

As I walked past the batting cages and into the dugout, Megan and the crew from *E:60* were there to meet me. Jeff Swinger was there too. He was the photographer who had taken the original pictures of me as batboy and who had gone to Washington, D.C. with us. He was like a big brother to me, which was good, since my brother, David, couldn't be there this year.

I saw Todd going down the steps to the locker room, and I ran over and fist-bumped him. He stopped and gave me a hug, saying, "I'm going to be hot today because of you. I'm going to get a couple of knocks for you. I love you, brother."

"I love you, too!" I said.

Mom and Dad were at the game, and I waved at them before the Reds took the field.

Then Dusty came up to the dugout and squeezed my shoulders. "Let's go tonight!"

I said, "Yeah, let's go, baby!"

Dusty handed me the starting lineup card and said, "Come with me. You know what to do." As I started out of the dugout, the PA announcer at GAPB announced my name. Fans cheered even louder than the first time I was batboy!

I took the lineup card to home plate to meet the Marlins manager and the game umpires. I even knew some of the umpires from the game last August, and they remembered me. The home plate umpire even said, "Hi, Teddy, how are you?" He patted me on the shoulder. I was really surprised.

Once I was back in the dugout, Luke reviewed everything about the bats in case I forgot and reminded me about taking the weighted bats and rosin bags to the on-deck circle. We talked about watching the umpire to see how many balls he needed at home plate and when to get the bats.

Soon it was time to sing the National Anthem. On the field, I stood between Todd and Dusty. Chris Heisey was on the other side of Dusty. After the National Anthem, we all went back into the dugout to get ready for the game. I yelled, "Good luck, everyone!"

Dusty said, "We don't need any more luck. We have you, Teddy!"

The game started and I was very busy with my batboy jobs, taking care of the on-deck circle during innings, getting bats for players, and putting bats in the correct places. I took balls to the plate umpire. Sometimes between innings I took him bottles of water. I wasn't so busy that I couldn't keep an eye on the game. Todd Frazier struck out in the bottom of the second inning. I told Todd, "That's okay. I still love you." He smiled at me and put his bat in the rack.

Then the Reds got a run in the third, and eight more in the fourth and fifth innings. In the sixth inning we were winning nine to one. It was great, and I raised my fist to the sky every time we scored. We were killing them. Tony Cringrani was sure striking out a lot of Marlins. He had eight strikeouts by the sixth inning. We were only three strikeouts from everyone in the stadium receiving a free La Rosa's pizza. All it takes is eleven! I was cheering as much for that as anything. After running back and forth picking up the bats and taking balls to the umpire, pizza sounded really good.

In the bottom of the sixth inning, Todd was up again and I walked up next to him at the steps and said, "Hey, Todd."

Todd said, "What's up?"

I said, "I love you, man."

"Really, I love you too, brother."

Then I said, "Hit a home run!"

Todd said, "You got it, Buddy."

Todd went up to bat as they played his theme song, "Fly Me to the Moon." I now have it as my cell phone ring. Jay Bruce was on first. Todd swung at the first pitch and missed it. He stepped out for a second and then got ready for the next pitch. I held my breath as the pitcher threw the ball. Todd swung and it sounded like a firecracker going off. He hit the ball really high and really far. The center fielder stood and watched it sail over his head. It kept going and going before it landed over the fence in center field. He had hit a home run! I started jumping up and down in the dugout. Jay Bruce came in to score and he motioned for me to come up to home plate to meet Todd. Then Chris Heisey yelled for me to go up to home plate.

I ran out to the plate. I was so excited, I even didn't check with Luke to see if it was okay.

I met Todd at home and was jumping all around. As we went back to the dugout, the umpire yelled for me to come back and get Todd's bat. He even handed it to me, but he was smiling. I'm the batboy and I forgot the bat! The Reds television announcer Tom Brennaman said Frazier's ball went 421 feet. That's a long way. I couldn't believe it then, and I still can't believe it today. One of my favorite players hit a homerun for me. I will never forget that moment.

Tom Brennaman told the television audience, "Teddy's more excited than Todd is!"

In the dugout I put Todd's bat away and ran down to see Todd again. He gave me a huge bear hug; in fact, he picked me up. He has to be really strong to do that!

Megan and the *E:60* crew seemed really happy with the way the game was going. To be honest, I even forgot they were there. I did see Megan talking to my mom. The weeks leading up to the game, Mom told Megan that she didn't think it would be possible to recreate my first night at batboy. Megan kept saying, "Let's see." Once Todd hit the home run, Megan couldn't stop smiling. The Reds struck out eleven Marlins, and all the fans received a certificate for a free pizza.

After the game, I got the shock of my life. Jim Day, the dugout reporter from *Reds Live*, told me that Jeff Piecora, another reporter from *Reds Live*, wanted to interview Todd and me. *Reds Live* is a television show that airs before and after the games. Jeff always interviews the star of the game on the field. Usually, he interviews the players, coaches, or Dusty. Not only does *Reds Live* air on television, it is shown on the big screen at the ballpark.

During the interview Jeff asked me, "What do you like about being batboy?"

I answered, "I like being with the players and the fans. I'm so happy we got a win for the team."

Jeff then asked, "What did you say to Todd before the home run?"

"I told Todd he and I were best friends. Hit a home run for me."

Jeff turned to Todd, "It doesn't get any better than this, does it?"

Todd said, "No, it doesn't! Teddy puts a smile on my face. He is one of my good buddies and is our good luck charm. We always win by nine or ten runs when he is here. We need him here more."

Later MLB posted online some really nice things that Reds shortstop Zach Cozart said about me.

"Teddy is awesome," Zach said. "This is the second time he's been batboy since I've been here. He just brings a lot of joy. He's always happy. He's running around telling everybody, 'Great job.' He's telling Frazier to hit a home run and Frazier does it. It's little stuff like that—he keeps the dugout pretty positive."

After the interview, I went to the locker room to change my clothes. I was still feeling great! I met my parents and Megan in front of the Diamond Club. Megan told my parents that I had asked Todd to hit a home run for me. Mom said, "Oh, no, you didn't!"

I just smiled and said, "Yes, and he did!"

Megan couldn't wait to check the tape. She was hoping that she caught it all on film. She said, "The game was like a Disney movie with the perfect ending—and it was all true."

The next morning there were lots of news stories about me, or as Jeff Swinger says, "There was a Teddy Explosion!" I never dreamed I would be on *Sports Center*, the show I watch everyday. David and Erin called about 7:15 and told us that while they were getting Trey and Cord ready for school, three-year-old Cord said, "Mommy, Teddy is on *Sports Center*. Why is Teddy on television?"

Erin ran into the family room and rewound the show. She yelled for David and Trey to come watch the show. They watched it again and then called right away. My brother said his phone wouldn't stop ringing. All his friends from college and work were calling him.

During the day, Megan called to tell me that I was going to be on *ABC World News Tonight* that evening. Diane Sawyer had seen me on *Sports Center* that morning and started to cry. Ms. Sawyer told Megan, "I need to have Teddy's story on my evening news tonight."

The phone rang all day long. Friends and people who barely knew us called to congratulate me. During one of those phone calls, Mom found out that some of my former classmates from Colerain were texting each other about me during the game. She said they were sharing high school memories about me. I bet some of them were pretty funny.

On the Saturday after the April 18 game, George Grant, another Reds announcer, was still showing clips of Thursday's game with Todd Frazier and me. He talked about my being from White Oak and loving the Reds! That evening we went to 4:30 Mass. I sat with my parents in the pew at the side of the church where we always sit. Father Bob Goebel was having Mass that day. He was standing next to the altar, and before he started Mass he wanted to recognize the student leaders from Our Lady of Grace School. He turned and looked over towards me and said he also wanted to recognize the Reds batboy, Teddy Kremer. He had me stand up and every person in church applauded. Talk about being surprised! After Mass, Father Goebel said his priest friends were talking about and wondering where I went to church. He just smiled at them and said, "Teddy goes to my church, little flower."

Chapter 20

AFTER MY APPEARANCE ON *SPORTS CENTER*, I WAS INVITED TO speak and participate at events all around Cincinnati. I was even invited to speak in Chicago and Indianapolis. Spring was busier than ever. I threw out the opening pitch for the Miracle League. Joe Nuxhall, a Cincinnati baseball pitcher and announcer, started the Miracle League to allow children with disabilities to play baseball. The baseball field is really cool; it's made of a rubber material so kids won't get hurt on the field. The rubber turf also helps kids with wheelchairs get around better.

After that I spoke at the Project SEARCH International Conference. One man in the audience said he was from Milwaukee and asked, "How about you coming to the Brewers and being the batboy?"

I answered with a straight face, "Next question, please?" Everyone laughed.

One night, Mom received a call from Michael LaRosa. He invited me to have dinner at LaRosa's Pizzeria on Boudinot Avenue. He also invited 25 of my friends and family to join me. The Reds mascots were even there! He served all kinds of pizza and my favorite, pepperoni and banana peppers. Michael LaRosa made it a special night for me. And guess who was managing LaRosa's that night—the man whose car I wrecked with Coach Newton's gator! I was really embarrassed to see him. Mom and Dad finally had a good laugh about it. It only took them about ten years!

In June my mom received a call from Patrick Leahy of the Cincinnati Reds. He told my mom that Phil Castellini had brought up my name at his weekly meeting and wanted a volunteer to find a place for me in the Reds organization. Patrick Leahy volunteered to be the "point man," as he called it. He contacted my parents and asked if I would be interested in working for the Reds. Of course I said, "YES, YES, YES!" I knew it would not be as the full time batboy, but at least I would be working for my favorite team!

Mr. Leahy told my mom that Jan Koshover would contact us and set something up. When Jan called, she told us that they would try me in a number of positions in the guest relations department and see which one was the best fit for me. We went to the ballpark in early July. Jan told me to wear khaki shorts and a Reds golf shirt. I met Mary Anne and Rob at Gapper Ally. They were the supervisors of the Guest Relations Department. Mary Anne showed us around. She was going to take to me to different jobs to see what I liked best. First Mary Ann took me to the front gates of GABP. A man named Ted taught me how to scan the tickets as the fans come through the gate. I scanned the fans' tickets. Some people wanted their picture taken with me, which really slowed down the line at the ballpark's entrance.

Next I worked the elevators and took the sports writers to the media floor. I took fans down to the Diamond Club and fans up to their seats on the fourth floor or to the box seat floor. Then I went to Fan Accommodations, which is part of the guest relations department. In Fan Accommodations, my job would be to type certificates for fans that have birthdays, catch foul balls, or are at GABP for the first time. I would also give out scorecards, verify "all you can eat" tickets, and sell future ball game tickets.

I liked all the jobs I tried, but when Jan called the next day, she said the best fit for me was Fan Accommodations. She then offered me the job and I accepted. I was to work for the Reds in the evening, Saturdays and Sundays. I still worked at Hillcrest three days a week. My mom and dad continued to drive me to horseback riding, private dancing lessons, softball, and swimming on my free days. I was really busy and my parents were even busier.

The first day I went to work for the Reds we had to go to the ballpark early to complete some paperwork and have my Reds badge made. I can't say I was really nervous about working for the Reds, but I was very excited. We were in Jan Koshover's office and she gave me the Reds Game Day Handbook. I needed to wear my badge and have my handbook with me at each game.

Rob came to get me from Jan's office and I was off to my job as a member of the Fan Accommodations team. Rob and Mary Ann helped me get started. Rob stayed with me for the first few innings to make sure everything was going well. The Reds invited my parents to the first few games. They wanted them to feel comfortable with me working in such a huge place. I felt fine but they worry a lot.

After my first few weeks on the job, Mom told Dad that she couldn't keep going to every game. She was still working full time as an instructional specialist for Northwest Local Schools. Dad worked for graduate services part time, but since he worked with schools, he had more free time in the summer. That meant Dad could go to the games with me. He had to take me down and pick me up anyway. Even though I knew how to ride the Metro, I didn't want to ride that late at night.

Dad had to buy tickets to all the games, and it was getting expensive. He asked Jan if he could help or volunteer—he was willing to pass out bobble heads or even sweep floors. Jan told him they didn't have volunteer positions, but they were going to need help when the college students went back to work. So Dad applied and the Reds hired him as an access coordinator. As Phil Castellini said, "We had to hire Dave so Teddy would have a chauffer."

I didn't think things could get any better than working for the Reds, but that summer my parents received a call from Topps, the company that makes baseball cards for MLB. We were eating lunch at the kitchen table when the phone rang. My mom went into the dining room to talk, so I knew it was an important call. The gentleman from Topps said he wanted to print a baseball card with me on it. My parents were really surprised and so was I! The gentleman said he would e-mail a picture that he planned to use on the card. Dusty Baker had requested to be on the card with me. And that was really cool! He also said I would be one of the few people who was not an MLB player, manager, or coach to be on a baseball card. The baseball card would be what Topps called a super-short print—they would only make fifty cards to be distributed throughout the United States.

One day in August, while Dad and I were working at the GABP, the Reds were really struggling, losing the game 15-2. When I got home, my mom said she had received a phone call in the 8th inning. It was Rick Stowe. "The Reds are struggling here today," he said to Mom.

My mom said, "I know. I'm watching and listening to it on TV."

Rick then said, "I am calling to get Teddy to come back to the dugout on Tuesday night."

"Rick, he is working in Fan Accommodations, remember?"

"I know, but being in the clubhouse as the batboy trumps all the other jobs in the ballpark!" He laughed. "Mr. Castellini wants him back."

When Dad and I arrived home that evening, Mom told me the news. I high-fived her and danced all around the living room. I would be back in the dugout! I couldn't wait. I got all my clothes ready, even my Nike shirt.

ON TUESDAY SECURITY LET US THROUGH Gapper's Ally again. Diana met us and we went down the ramp to the clubhouse entrance. I walked into the clubhouse office; Luke was there to meet me. He said, "I'm glad you're back, Teddy!"

He took me back to where he and I could dress. As usual, Luke had to help me get my socks on. He was always there to help me or tell me I could do it. Of course, he sometimes had to hurry me along in the clubhouse when I stopped to talk to my baseball friends.

Dusty saw me and said he was glad I was back. "We could use some of your luck," he said. I told him his "good luck charm" was back and that I would do my best! He told me to meet him in the dugout to take the lineup card out again.

I was glad to see all the players in the clubhouse. Todd Frazier and Chris Heisey came up to me right away. Brandon Philips came over and gave a hug. Chris Heisey gave me his red, white, and blue Phiten necklace to wear. Almost all the players were wearing them. I was so happy and gave Chris a big hug.

I went out to the dugout and waved to my parents. My friend Sean Jones was sitting with them. Then Dusty came into the dugout and asked, "Are you ready for another game?"

"Always!" I shouted. We went to home plate to exchange the lineup cards with the manager of the Oakland Athletics. I talked to the umpire, John Hirscheck, and he knew who I was. Every time I took balls or water out to him during innings, he would talk to me like I was an old friend.

My jobs in the dugout were the same. I was really getting good at carrying the bats and rosin bags from the dugout to the on-deck circle. I didn't feel like I was going to drop everything. I guess practice does make perfect or almost perfect. Brandon, Todd, and Jay Bruce all talked to me before they went up to bat. The fans cheered each time I came out on the field to take water or balls to the umpire.

At the beginning of the seventh inning, Luke said to me, "I think you've got this. I'm going to change out of my uniform. I'll be right back. Okay?"

I shooed him away, and said, "Sure, go ahead, I've got this." Now, the team and the dugout were all mine. I couldn't believe that Luke trusted me that much and let me take over as batboy. He didn't feel like he had to be dressed out in case something went wrong. Of course, my mom and dad noticed that when Luke came back he was in his street clothes. Now that he was out of uniform, Luke couldn't go out on the field again. I guess this freaked my parents out, because my dad left the stands and came down to ask Luke what was going on.

Luke smiled and said, "Teddy's doing fine. He doesn't need me. He knows what to do, but I'll stay just in case. Don't worry, he'll be fine."

We beat the Athletics 3-1. Matt Latos was the winning pitcher. At the end of the game, I walked out on the field with the team to shake hands. John Hirscheck, the umpire, called me over and told me I did a really great job. It was a very special night. Brian Giesenschlag from *Reds Live* interviewed Jay Bruce as the star of the game. When I was walking back with the players, Brian called me over to do an interview. I told Brian I was thrilled that the Reds won the game, and that I wanted them to keep winning. Brian asked, "How many wins is this for you as the batboy?"

"This is my third win, Brian. I am honored to be here as the Reds good luck charm." As I was talking to him, I noticed that I was on the big screen. Wow!

Brian asked me if I would be back in the dugout. I told him I would be back if they needed me. I would be waiting for the phone call.

After the game Mom and Dad told me that Pete Rose—"The Hit King"—was at the game. Wow! I thought. Pete Rose! I hoped he thought I did a good job. Pete comes to the Reds games whenever he is in town. He was part of the Big Red Machine along with Johnny Bench, Tony Perez, and Dave Concepcion. They are one of my favorite Reds teams, even though I wasn't born yet when they were playing. Or as Dad says, "Not even a twinkle in his eye."

I asked after the game if Pete was still there, because I wanted to meet him and shake his hand. But by the time I got off the field and changed, Pete was gone.

My parents said that some Korean gentlemen were sitting in the seats behind them. Even though they spoke mostly Korean, they told Mom they had come to see Reds player Shin-Soo Choo. Then the men pointed to me saying, "Teddy." Somehow they figured out that Mom and Dad knew me. They smiled and asked Mom, "Teddy?"

My mom said, "Yes."

"How long?" they asked.

It took a while, but finally Mom figured out what they were asking. "Thirty years old," she replied.

"We like Teddy's smile," they said.

Later, these same men were watching all the people lining up in the aisle next to the Diamond Club seats between innings. The people were passing balls and programs over to Pete Rose for autographs. The Korean gentlemen tapped my dad on the shoulder and asked, "Who?" They were pointing to Pete Rose.

My dad tried to explain who Pete Rose was. He said that he was called "The Hit King." They shrugged. Then the men pulled out a tablet and Googled Pete Rose and showed it to my dad.

Dad said, "Yes, that's him!" They just smiled and shook their heads. Then they took pictures of Pete and me. Next, they wanted autographs. My parents thought it was funny that the Korean gentlemen knew me and not Pete Rose.

That was quite a night!

Epilogue

THE REDS FIRED DUSTY BAKER ON OCT 4, 2013, AND I WAS REALLY sad. I cried when I heard it on TV. He was so nice to me, and I will always keep the lineup card he gave me framed on my bedroom wall. I have all my wonderful memories of how he allowed me to be part of the team. He always made me feel welcome.

One Monday in late October as I was getting ready for horseback riding, the phone rang and I answered it. A familiar voice asked for Cheryl and I handed my mom the phone. I whispered to my mom, "I know that voice, but I can't think of who it is." As I walked to my room to get my jeans, boots, and helmet, I could hear my mom talking excitedly into the phone. I finally remembered whose voice it was. I ran back into the kitchen to see if I was right. My mom gave me the phone and whispered, "It's Dusty Baker."

I was right! I told Dusty, "I miss you and I still love you."

Dusty said, "Well, I love you too, Teddy." He asked, "How are you doing?"

"I really miss you. I can't believe you aren't going to manage the Reds anymore."

He said, "I really miss you, too, and I know I'm really going to miss the Reds. In this business, managers are let go all the time. Winning is everything."

He asked, "What's your schedule for tonight?" I told him that I had horseback riding.

Dusty then said, "Now, Teddy, be sure you don't fall off that animal!"

"Dusty, it's a horse." We laughed and he said, "Just be careful."

He asked to talk to my mom again. Dusty told Mom that if I ever needed anything not to hesitate to call him, and that if he came to town we would get together.

Mom thanked him for all he did for the Reds and for me. He gave my mom his phone number and address. He said if I ever traveled out west, I should visit him. Before he got off the phone, Dusty told my mom that when he was growing up his mother worked with special needs children, and he often played baseball with her students. They loved hitting the ball and playing catch. He told my mom that he enjoyed being with me and that I would always be his good luck charm.

IN 2015 I WAS THE HONORARY Grand Marshall for the Opening Day parade. It was fun to sit in the back of a nice car and wave at people. I am still thrilled that people know how much I love the Reds.

The All-Star game was in Cincinnati that same year. My parents and I went to the Homerun Derby the day before the game. Todd Frazier was in it and no one even mentioned him as a favorite to win. Guess who was cheering for him like crazy the whole time— Me! Even Todd was excited when he hit the last homer to win it all. At the big game, I continued to work in Fan Accommodations, and I met people from all over the world. It was amazing!

In the All-Star game Todd started at third base. Millions of people saw my favorite player, and friend, play baseball. It was great. Before the game, the most famous players from my dad's days were there. I saw Hank Aaron, Sandy Koufax, Willie Mays, and Reds catcher Johnny Bench. Then they called other really old Reds players out to the field. One of them was Pete Rose. It was a pretty good All-Star game for my team and for my hometown.

IN EARLY DECEMBER OF 2015 THE Reds held their annual Redsfest, and the Reds gave us tickets. Sometimes I work at the event, but that year I just was a fan. While there, Dad and I ran into Karen Forgus, Senior Vice President of Business Operations. She asked, "Who do you want to see?"

"Todd, of course!"

She took me to the front of the line at Todd's signing table. He jumped up and gave me a huge hug and we talked for a while. The fans in line didn't mind; they were all taking pictures of Todd and me. I didn't know that would be the last time I would see Todd as a Cincinnati Red. It makes me sad every time I think about it. Did you know that every time Todd hit a home run, he would point up to the fourth floor as he crossed the plate? The Fan Accommodations booth was on the fourth floor, and Todd knew I would be watching him. The people in Fan Accommodations would always say, "Go on out, Teddy!" So I would run to the top of stairs, look down, and point back at Todd.

A week and a half later, I was watching the MLB network on Wednesday, December 16 and was shocked to learn that the Reds had traded Todd to the Chicago White Sox. They are in the American League, and the White Sox are not even on the Reds schedule. What a bummer. I was really upset about the trade and couldn't stop crying.

That afternoon my mom started receiving phone calls from television stations. Channel 9 wanted to come to our house and interview me about the trade. My parents were having company that evening, but my mom said yes. Then Channel 12 called and wanted to come, too.

Channel 9 wanted an interview with my *E:60* DVD playing in the background. I was fine for the first part of the interview, but when I saw the part in the *E:60* film of Todd hitting his famous home run, I broke down and started to cry again. Dad put his arm around me, and even he had tears in his eyes. So did my mom. The reporters and film crew even started to tear up. It was a sad time for Cincinnati.

After they left, Channel 12 came to the house. Brad Underwood interviewed me. He asked how I felt and I told him, "Really sad." I started to cry again. What a terrible day.

EVEN THOUGH THE REDS TRADED TODD FRAZIER, I still love them. Being batboy for the Reds has changed my world, and I'm thankful for all the opportunities they gave me, an ordinary guy with Down syndrome. I met so many great people along the way, but I will never forget the day I met a little girl from Indiana while I was a Goodwill Ambassador for the Reds.

I had only been working a few weeks and during the games, I worked on the top floor in the fan booth. But before the games, I often stood out by the front gates and greeted people. That particular day a mom and dad walked up with their daughter. The mom told me her little girl was ten years old and her name was Elizabeth. Elizabeth stared at me for a minute and then reached out and hugged me. She wouldn't let go and her mother started to cry. Her mother said, "Ever since we heard your story, Teddy, we have saved up so we could come to a game. We wanted Elizabeth to never give up. You have made her feel better about herself." She laid her hand on her daughter's shoulder and looked me in the eyes. "We can't thank you enough."

Elizabeth had Down syndrome, just like me. I didn't know what to say at first, but then I looked at Elizabeth and said, "I love you." She finally let go and the family walked into the game. I watched them for a moment and then other fans started to shake my hand. I never saw Elizabeth again, but I'm glad I met her.

People like Elizabeth make it easy for me to feel closer to God. When I think about what God means, I sometimes see people looking for Him in places they can't reach. But to me, I have seen God in the eyes of my friend Tommy on the Unified Softball field, and in the eyes of my friend Todd Frazier, and in the eyes of Elizabeth.

I have always felt love for others. I may not have every emotion just like everyone else does, but I think that's okay. If I had to have just one emotion, it would be love. I think I had that from my very first moment on the day I was born. I have always felt loved by my family. I know they have helped me in ways I can never understand. And never repay. And so have many other people. My coaches cheered me on in the pool and on the field; my teachers always had faith in me; my friends made me feel special and accepted; and the Reds showed the world what an ordinary guy with Down syndrome can do. I love them all for loving me so much.

And that makes me love my life with all my heart.

Teddy (age 22) gets sworn in for his first job at the Hillcrest court house

Teddy (age 23) riding Tin Man

Teddy (age 28) riding Chevy

Brandon Phillips with Teddy, first time as batboy, 2012
(Photo courtesy of *Cincinnati Enquirer* photojournalist Jeff Swinger)

First time as batboy, 2012
(Photo courtesy of *Cincinnati Enquirer* photojournalist Jeff Swinger)

Post game with Dusty, 2012
(Photo courtesy of *Cincinnati Enquirer* photojournalist Jeff Swinger)

Teddy and Chris Heisey, 2012
(Photo courtesy of *Cincinnati Enquirer* photojournalist Jeff Swinger)

Teddy and Dusty, 2012
(Photo courtesy of *Cincinnati Enquirer* photojournalist Jeff Swinger)

Teddy (age 30), first time as batboy
(Photo courtesy of *Cincinnati Enquirer* photojournalist Jeff Swinger)

Teddy (age 30) with family in Disney World

Teddy gives a fist pump, third time as batboy, 2013
(Photo courtesy of *Cincinnati Enquirer* photojournalist Jeff Swinger)

Todd Fraizer hits a home run for Teddy, 2013
(Photo courtesy of *Cincinnati Enquirer* photojournalist Jeff Swinger)

Teddy embraces Todd Fraizer after the home run
(Photo courtesy of *Cincinnati Enquirer* photojournalist Jeff Swinger)

Teddy receives Colerain's Distinguished Alumni Award, 2013

Teddy and Mary dancing to "Fly Me to the Moon"

Footwork of "Fly me to the Moon"

Teddy (age 31) with Todd, second time as batboy
(Photo courtesy of *Cincinnati Enquirer* photojournalist Jeff Swinger)

Teddy (age 31) in a commercial for Cincinnati Octoberfest

Teddy and Bill Hemmer, Spirit of Cincinnati Award, 2014

Teddy and Michael Annett, Daytona Firecracker Race, 2014

Teddy and Todd Frazier at Reel Abilities, 2014
(Photo courtesy of *Cincinnati Enquirer* photojournalist Jeff Swinger)

Grand Marshall Teddy, Opening Day 2014
(Photo courtesy of *Cincinnati Enquirer* photojournalist Jeff Swinger)

Grand Marshall Teddy, Opening Day 2014
(Photo courtesy of *Cincinnati Enquirer* photojournalist Jeff Swinger)

Teddy visits Sister Martha in Louisville, 2014

Todd Frazier surprises Teddy at Reel Abilities, 2014
(Photo courtesy of *Cincinnati Enquirer* photojournalist Jeff Swinger)

Teddy's name on Michael Annett's car at Indianapolis Brickyard Race

Family Christmas tree cutting at Butler Tree Farm, Christmas 2015

Storytellers forum, All Star Game 2015
(Photo courtesy of *Cincinnati Enquirer* photojournalist Jeff Swinger)

Teddy and Sister Aloyse, 2015

Teddy receives an award from Fifth Third, 2015

Teddy visits Santa at Butler Tree Farm, 2015

Teddy (Age 32) at the Ohio Public Image Award with Mitch Morgan and
Shirlene Gibbs, 2015

Teddy (age 32) and Sean Jones at Reel Abilities Film Festival

Teddy welcomes visitors to Cincinnati for the All Star Game

Co-workers gave Teddy a bobble head

Awards and Participations

Reel Abilities Film Festival 2015, Honorary Co-Chair, February 27-March 7
Joe Nuxhall Miracle League Ball, Host and Greeter, 2014, 2015
The Point of Northern Kentucky , Spokesman, 2013 to present
The Point Annual Fund Raiser, Guest Auctioneer , 2013, 2014, 2015
Reel Abilities Out Reach Educational Program at High Schools and Junior
    High Schools, presenter, 2013 to present
Cincinnati Rotary Club Fundraiser, Guest Auctioneer, 2014, 2015
Rusty Ball Fundraiser, VIP/ Guest Auctioneer, 2014, 2015,

Reds Honors

Finley Market Opening Day Parade, the Enquirer Car, 2013
Participated in the Reds Opening Night, walked the red carpet, 2013
Finley Market Opening Day Parade Honorary Grand Marshall, 2014
Honorary Captain for Reds Opening Day, 2015
Cincinnati Reds, Bat Boy, August 17, 2012, April 18, 2013, August 6, 2013
Invited to the Brick Yard 500 Race, name placed on Michael Annette's car, 2014
Guest of Former Speaker of the House John Boehner at the State of the Union
    Address, 2014
Spirit of Cincinnati USA Award, Ambassador Award, 2013
Colerain High School Distinguished Alumni Award, 2013
Grand Marshall of Aurora Opening Day Parade For Knothole Baseball, 2014
Down Sydrome Association of Western Michigan, Guest Speaker, 2014
NADS Conference "Dare to Dream", Guest Speaker, 2014

Teddy's Co-Authors

MICHAEL BUCHANAN AND DIANE Lang latest co-authored novel, *The Fat Boy Chronicles*, was released in 2010. The book won the National Parenting Publication's Gold Award, and Mom's Choice Award of Excellence and is used by schools around the nation in their anti-bullying and childhood obesity efforts. The authors won the NY Champions of Character Award for Literature in 2013. The writing team were the writers for the feature documentary *Spiral Bound*, a film about the importance of the arts in our communities and nation. This film will premiere in Charlotte, NC, in September of 2014.

Buchanan and Lang also wrote the screenplay for the feature film *The Fat Boy Chronicles*. During its festival tour, the movie won multiple awards for its impacting, yet hopeful depiction of an obese and bullied 9th grader's world. Upon the film's release in early 2012, it quickly rose to #6 family rental in Redbox and has now been seen by several million people on Netflix.

The co-authors are guest speakers at schools nationwide as well as state and national conferences where they discuss the connection between bullying, childhood obesity, and school climate. Buchanan was a featured speaker at the 2011 International Anti-Bullying Convention in New Orleans. Both nationally-recognized retired teachers, the pair conduct screenwriting workshops in schools as well as speaking at various writing conferences.

The sequel to *The Fat Boy Chronicles* is underway while their new Tween book, *Treasure of the Four Lions*, is completed. In development are their feature length screenplays *Bait and Tackle* and *Treasure of the Four Lions*. Other produced films are the shorts *Last Bullet* and *Boxes*, both of which won multiple awards on the festival circuit.

Their latest novel, *Under the Gumbo Limbo Tree*, was released by Deeds Publishing in April 2016.

Buchanan lives in Alpharetta, Georgia, while Lang resides in Cincinnati, Ohio.

CPSIA information can be obtained at www.ICGtesting.com
Printed in the USA
LVOW10s1353080616

491755LV00017B/158/P